PHILADELPHIA

Busy Family Recipes

pil

Publications International, Ltd.

Pictured on the front cover: Creamy Zucchini & Spinach Rigatoni *(page 108)*.
Pictured on the back cover (clockwise from top): Grilled Tomato Salsa Appetizers *(page 8)*, Lemon Tropical Pound Cake *(page 116),* and Seafood Enchiladas *(page 60)*.

ISBN-13: 978-1-4508-2486-6
ISBN-10: 1-4508-2486-2

Library of Congress Control Number: 2011923871

Manufactured in China.

8 7 6 5 4 3 2 1

Microwave Cooking: Microwave ovens vary in wattage. Use the cooking times as guidelines and check for doneness before adding more time.

Preparation/Cooking Times: Preparation times are based on the approximate amount of time required to assemble the recipe before cooking, baking, chilling, or serving. These times include preparation steps such as measuring, chopping, and mixing. The fact that some preparations and cooking can be done simultaneously is taken into account. Preparation of optional ingredients and serving suggestions is not included.

contents

Welcome to PHILADELPHIA Cream Cheese Busy Family Recipes, your answer to the daily dilemma of "what's for dinner?" Whether you need a classic never-fail dessert, a make-ahead snack, or a crowd-pleasing casserole, we've got recipes for every taste, budget, and timetable.

Families on the go often need quick bites for after-school events. Try a variety of hot and cold dips, appetizers, and snacks like Make-Ahead Spinach Phyllo Roll-Ups, Blue Cheese Mushrooms, 2-Minute Delicious PHILLY Dip, and Easy Layered Tomato Dip. Weeknight dinners are a snap with hearty one-dish meals and easy entrées like Potato-Topped Mini Meatloaves, White & Gold Pizza, Seafood Enchiladas, and Chicken & Pepper Pasta Bake.

Of course, every main meal needs tasty accompaniments. Find vegetable bakes, breads, and other side dishes like Crispy-Topped Creamy Spinach, Honey Cream Filled Crescents, Chive & Onion Mashed Potatoes, and Creamy Sweet Whipped Carrots that complete any menu. Wow family and friends with classic cheesecakes, cakes, and pies like Blossoming Berry Cheesecake, Lemon Tropical Pound Cake, Chocolate Silk Pie with Marshmallow Meringue, and Frozen Coconut Pie. We've even included a special section devoted to everyone's favorite flavor—chocolate! Warm & Gooey Peanut Butter-Chocolate Cake, Creamy Chocolate Bars, and So-Easy German Chocolate Cake are simple to make but hard to resist.

We've collected more than 90 family-pleasing favorites to enjoy all year long. Make mealtime a snap with fast, innovative, and delicious dishes made with America's favorite brand, PHILADELPHIA Cream Cheese.

Party Starters

A variety of hot and cold dips, appetizers, and snacks perfect for any get-together

blue cheese mushrooms

PREP: 30 min. | TOTAL: 33 min. | MAKES: about 2 doz. or 24 servings, 1 mushroom each.

▶ what you need!

1 lb. medium fresh mushrooms

¼ cup sliced green onions

1 Tbsp. butter or margarine

1 pkg. (4 oz.) ATHENOS Crumbled Blue Cheese

3 oz. PHILADELPHIA Cream Cheese, softened

▶ make it!

1. **HEAT** broiler. Remove stems from mushrooms; chop stems. Cook and stir stems and onions in butter in small skillet on medium heat until tender.

2. **ADD** blue cheese and cream cheese; mix well. Spoon evenly into mushroom caps; place on rack of broiler pan.

3. **BROIL** 2 to 3 min. or until golden brown. Serve warm.

grilled tomato salsa appetizers

PREP: 15 min. | TOTAL: 25 min. | MAKES: 24 servings, 1 appetizer each.

▶ what you need!

12 oz. (about 21) cherry tomatoes

1 small onion, quartered

1 jalapeño pepper

¼ cup KRAFT Zesty Italian Dressing, divided

4 oz. (½ of 8-oz. pkg.) PHILADELPHIA Cream Cheese, softened

2 Tbsp. KRAFT Grated Parmesan Cheese

1 Tbsp. chopped basil

1 French baguette, cut into 24 slices, toasted

▶ make it!

1. **HEAT** grill to medium-high heat. Mix tomatoes, onion, pepper and 2 Tbsp. of the dressing in medium bowl. Mix cream cheese and Parmesan cheese in separate bowl until well blended; set aside.

2. **PLACE** tomatoes and onion on separate skewers. Place skewers and jalapeño pepper on grill grate. Grill 6 to 8 min. or until tender, turning every 2 min. and brushing with remaining 2 Tbsp. dressing.

3. **REMOVE** tomatoes and onion from skewers; chop onion. Seed and chop pepper. Mix tomatoes, onion, pepper and basil with fork until tomatoes are chunky.

4. **SPREAD** each baguette slice with cream cheese mixture. Top with tomato mixture. Serve warm or cold.

SUBSTITUTE:
Prepare as directed, using KRAFT Light Italian Dressing and PHILADELPHIA Neufchâtel Cheese.

HOW TO HANDLE FRESH CHILE PEPPERS:
When handling fresh chile peppers, be sure to wear disposable rubber or clear plastic gloves to avoid irritating your skin. Never touch your eyes, nose or mouth when handling the peppers. If you've forgotten to wear the gloves and feel a burning sensation in your hands, apply a baking soda and water paste to the affected area. After rinsing the paste off, you should feel some relief.

smoked salmon cheesecake

PREP: 15 min. | TOTAL: 5 hours 15 min. | MAKES: 40 servings, 2 Tbsp. each.

▶ what you need!

1 cup dry bread crumbs

3 Tbsp. butter or margarine, melted

3 pkg. (8 oz. each) PHILADELPHIA Cream Cheese, softened

4 eggs

½ lb. smoked salmon, chopped

½ cup green onion slices

2 to 3 Tbsp. chopped fresh dill

NABISCO Crackers and sliced fresh vegetables

▶ make it!

1. **HEAT** oven to 325°F if using a silver 9-inch springform pan (or to 300°F if using a dark nonstick 9-inch springform pan.) Mix bread crumbs and butter; press firmly onto bottom of pan. Bake 10 min.

2. **BEAT** cream cheese in large bowl with electric mixer on medium speed until creamy. Add eggs, 1 at a time, mixing on low speed after each addition just until blended. Stir in remaining ingredients. Pour over crust.

3. **BAKE** 1 hour or until center is almost set. Run knife or metal spatula around rim of pan to loosen cake; cool before removing rim of pan. Refrigerate 4 hours or overnight. Let stand 15 min. at room temperature before serving. Serve with your favorite NABISCO Crackers and fresh vegetables.

SUBSTITUTE:
Prepare as directed, using PHILADELPHIA Neufchâtel Cheese.

HOW TO SOFTEN CREAM CHEESE:
Place completely unwrapped pkg. of cream cheese in microwaveable bowl. Microwave on HIGH 15 to 20 sec. or until slightly softened.

easy-bake cheese & pesto

PREP: 10 min. | TOTAL: 40 min. | MAKES: 12 servings.

▶ what you need!

1 can (4 oz.) reduced-fat refrigerated crescent dinner rolls

1 pkg. (8 oz.) PHILADELPHIA Neufchâtel Cheese

2 Tbsp. pesto

2 Tbsp. chopped roasted red peppers

1 egg, lightly beaten

RITZ Reduced Fat Crackers

▶ make it!

1. **HEAT** oven to 350°F. Unroll dough on lightly greased baking sheet; firmly press seams together to form 12×4-inch rectangle.

2. **CUT** Neufchâtel horizontally in half with sharp knife. Place 1 of the Neufchâtel pieces on half of dough; top with 1 Tbsp. of the pesto and the peppers. Cover with remaining Neufchâtel piece; spread top with remaining 1 Tbsp. pesto. Brush dough with egg; fold dough in half to completely enclose filling. Press edges of dough together to seal. Brush top with any remaining egg.

3. **BAKE** 15 to 18 min. or until lightly browned. Cool 10 min. Serve with RITZ Reduced Fat Crackers.

MAKE AHEAD:
Assemble on baking sheet as directed. Cover and refrigerate up to 4 hours. When ready to serve, uncover and bake as directed.

NUTRITION BONUS:
This tasty appetizer, made with better-for-you ingredients, can fit into a healthful eating plan.

make-ahead spinach phyllo roll-ups

PREP: 30 min. | TOTAL: 55 min. | MAKES: 30 servings or 5 logs, 6 servings each.

▶ what you need!

1 egg, beaten

1 pkg. (10 oz.) frozen chopped spinach, thawed, drained

1 cup ATHENOS Traditional Crumbled Feta Cheese

1 tub (8 oz.) PHILADELPHIA Garden Vegetable ⅓ Less Fat than Cream Cheese

4 green onions, finely chopped

15 sheets frozen phyllo (14×9 inch), thawed

⅓ cup butter, melted

▶ make it!

1. **MIX** first 5 ingredients until well blended; set aside. Brush 1 phyllo sheet lightly with butter; top with 2 more phyllo sheets, lightly brushing each layer with some of the remaining butter. Place remaining phyllo between sheets of plastic wrap; set aside.

2. **SPREAD** ⅕ of the spinach mixture along 1 short side of phyllo stack; fold in both long sides then roll up, starting at 1 of the short sides to make log. Repeat with remaining phyllo sheets and spinach mixture to make 4 more logs. Brush with remaining butter. Make small cuts in tops of logs at 1-inch intervals. Place in large freezer-weight resealable plastic bags or wrap tightly in plastic wrap.

3. **FREEZE** up to 3 months. When ready to bake, remove desired number of logs from freezer. Refrigerate, tightly wrapped, several hours or overnight until thawed. Unwrap, then place on baking sheet. Bake in 375°F oven 25 min. or until golden brown. Cool on baking sheet 5 min.; transfer to cutting board. Use serrated knife to cut each log into 6 slices.

STORAGE KNOW-HOW:
Leftover phyllo sheets can be wrapped tightly and refrozen.

HOW TO PREPARE WITH 18×14-INCH PHYLLO SHEETS:
Use a total of 9 phyllo sheets, spreading ⅓ of the filling on each stack of 3 sheets and rolling up each stack to make a total of 3 logs. Freeze and bake as directed. Cut each log into 10 slices to serve.

VARIATION:
Omit butter. Spray phyllo sheets with cooking spray instead of brushing with the melted butter.

greek antipasto dip

PREP: 10 min. | TOTAL: 22 min. | MAKES: 2 cups dip or 16 servings, 2 Tbsp. dip and 16 crackers each.

▶ what you need!

1 pkg. (8 oz.) PHILADELPHIA Neufchâtel Cheese, softened

1 clove garlic, finely chopped

⅓ cup chopped roasted red peppers

¼ cup finely chopped red onions

1 Tbsp. olive oil

¼ cup ATHENOS Crumbled Reduced Fat Feta Cheese

½ small lemon, seeded

1 Tbsp. minced fresh parsley

WHEAT THINS Snack Crackers

▶ make it!

1. **HEAT** oven to 350°F. Mix Neufchâtel cheese and garlic; spread onto bottom of 9-inch pie plate.

2. **COVER** with peppers and onions. Drizzle with oil; sprinkle with feta cheese.

3. **BAKE** 10 to 12 min. or until heated through. Squeeze lemon over dip. Sprinkle with parsley. Serve with crackers.

SERVING SUGGESTION:
Serve with WHEAT THINS Big Snack Crackers.

garlic-shrimp cups

PREP: 35 min. | TOTAL: 1 hour 45 min. | MAKES: 2 doz. or 24 servings, 1 shrimp cup each.

▶ what you need!

   2 eggs

   ½ cup water

   24 TRISCUIT Roasted Garlic Crackers

   2 oz. (¼ of 8-oz. pkg.) PHILADELPHIA Neufchâtel Cheese, softened

   ¼ tsp. lemon peel

   2 tsp. lemon juice

   2 tsp. fat-free milk

   2 tsp. chopped fresh parsley

   24 uncooked medium shrimp (about ½ lb.), peeled, deveined

   2 cloves garlic, minced

▶ make it!

1. **HEAT** oven to 350°F. Beat eggs and water in pie plate with whisk until blended. Add 12 crackers; let stand 8 min., turning over after 4 min. Press 1 soaked cracker onto bottom and up side of each of 12 mini muffin pan cups sprayed with cooking spray. Repeat with remaining 12 crackers in additional muffin cups.

2. **BAKE** 8 to 10 min. or until lightly browned. Use metal spatula to carefully loosen crusts from muffin pan; transfer to lightly greased baking sheet. Bake an additional 20 to 25 min. or until crisp. Remove to wire racks; cool.

3. **MEANWHILE,** mix Neufchâtel cheese, lemon peel, lemon juice, milk and parsley; set aside. Cook and stir shrimp and garlic in nonstick skillet sprayed with cooking spray on medium-high heat 3 to 4 min. or until shrimp turn pink. Place 1 shrimp in each cracker cup; top with Neufchâtel cheese mixture.

MAKE AHEAD:
Cooled baked cracker cups can be stored in airtight container at room temperature up to 8 hours. Cooked shrimp and Neufchâtel cheese mixture can be stored in separate containers in refrigerator until ready to use. When ready to serve, place 1 shrimp in each cup; place on baking sheet. Bake at 350°F for 7 to 8 min. or until shrimp are heated through before topping with Neufchâtel mixture.

SHORTCUT:
In a hurry? Try this quick-and-easy variation instead. Omit eggs and water. Prepare Neufchâtel cheese mixture and cook shrimp as directed. Spread Neufchâtel cheese mixture onto crackers, then top with shrimp and sprinkle with parsley.

mini shrimp cocktail bites

PREP: 10 min. | TOTAL: 10 min. | MAKES: 8 servings, 2 topped crackers each.

▶ what you need!

16 RITZ or Holiday RITZ Crackers

⅓ cup PHILADELPHIA Whipped Cream Cheese Spread

⅓ cup KRAFT Cocktail Sauce

16 cleaned large fresh shrimp, cooked

⅓ cup finely chopped green onions

▶ make it!

1. **SPREAD** each cracker with 1 tsp. of the cream cheese spread.

2. **TOP** evenly with the cocktail sauce, shrimp and onions.

KEEPING IT SAFE:
Frozen shrimp can also be used to prepare these appetizers. To thaw the shrimp, place the bag of frozen shrimp in the refrigerator and let stand until thawed. Or, place the sealed bag of shrimp in a bowl of cold water and let stand until thawed, changing the water every 10 min. Never thaw the shrimp on the countertop.

chipotle chicken bites

▶ what you need!

2 Tbsp. KRAFT Zesty Italian Dressing

1 small whole chipotle pepper in adobo sauce, chopped

1 cup shredded cooked chicken breast

4 oz. (½ of 8-oz. pkg.) PHILADELPHIA Cream Cheese, softened

½ cup chopped mango

24 RITZ Crackers

2 Tbsp. finely chopped cilantro

▶ make it!

1. **PLACE** dressing and chipotle in blender; cover. Blend until smooth. Mix chicken and dressing mixture in small bowl.

2. **MIX** cream cheese and mango in separate small bowl until well blended.

3. **TOP** each cracker with about 1 tsp. cream cheese mixture and about 1 Tbsp. chicken mixture. Sprinkle with cilantro.

SUBSTITUTE:
Try cooked pork instead of the chicken.

SUBSTITUTE:
Instead of the mango, try fresh raspberries or ripe peaches when in season!

2-minute delicious PHILLY dip

PREP: 5 min. | TOTAL: 5 min. | MAKES: ½ cup dip or 4 servings, 2 Tbsp. dip and 3 crackers each.

▶ what you need!

¼ cup PHILADELPHIA Cream Cheese Spread

1 Tbsp. KRAFT CATALINA Dressing

2 Tbsp. sliced black olives

TRISCUIT Thin Crisps

▶ make it!

1. **MIX** first 3 ingredients until well blended.

2. **SERVE** with crackers.

VARIATION:
Serve with celery sticks instead of/in addition to the crackers.

SUBSTITUTE:
Prepare using green olives.

baked triple-veggie dip

PREP: 15 min. | **TOTAL:** 50 min. | **MAKES:** 4½ cups or 36 servings, 2 Tbsp. each.

▶ what you need!

1½ cups KRAFT Grated Parmesan Cheese, divided

1 can (1 lb. 3 oz.) asparagus spears, drained, chopped

1 pkg. (10 oz.) frozen chopped spinach, thawed, drained

1 can (8½ oz.) artichoke hearts, drained, chopped

1 container (8 oz.) PHILADELPHIA Chive & Onion Cream Cheese Spread

½ cup KRAFT Real Mayo Mayonnaise

▶ make it!

1. **HEAT** oven to 375°F.

2. **MIX** 1¼ cups Parmesan with all remaining ingredients.

3. **SPOON** into 2-qt. baking dish; top with remaining Parmesan.

4. **BAKE** 35 min. or until dip is heated through and top is lightly browned.

VARIATION:
Prepare as directed, using KRAFT Reduced Fat Parmesan Style Grated Topping, PHILADELPHIA Chive & Onion ⅓ Less Fat than Cream Cheese and KRAFT Mayo with Olive Oil Reduced Fat Mayonnaise.

NUTRITION BONUS:
The spinach is a good source of vitamin A in this tasty baked dip.

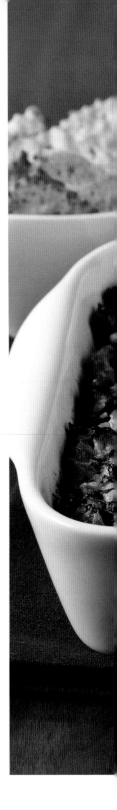

sun-dried tomato & garlic dip

PREP: 5 min. | TOTAL: 5 min. | MAKES: 2 cups or 16 servings, 2 Tbsp. each.

▶ what you need!

1 tub (8 oz.) PHILADELPHIA Cream Cheese Spread

½ cup MIRACLE WHIP Dressing

½ cup sun-dried tomatoes packed in oil, drained, chopped

2 Tbsp. finely chopped fresh chives

1 clove garlic, minced

1 tsp. black pepper

NABISCO Crackers or cut-up fresh vegetables

▶ make it!

1. **MIX** all ingredients until well blended.

2. **SERVE** with NABISCO Crackers or vegetables.

MAKE AHEAD:
This dip can be made up to 24 hours in advance. The longer you leave this dip in the refrigerator, the better the flavor.

tomato-basil dip

PREP: 10 min. | **TOTAL:** 10 min. | **MAKES:** 1¾ cups or 14 servings, 2 Tbsp. each.

▶ what you need!

1 pkg. (8 oz.) PHILADELPHIA Neufchâtel Cheese, softened

2 plum tomatoes, seeded, chopped

2 Tbsp. KRAFT Zesty Italian Dressing

2 Tbsp. KRAFT Shredded Parmesan Cheese

1 Tbsp. finely chopped fresh basil

WHEAT THINS Snack Crackers or cut-up fresh vegetables

▶ make it!

1. **SPREAD** Neufchâtel cheese onto bottom of 9-inch pie plate.

2. **MIX** tomatoes and dressing; spoon over Neufchâtel cheese. Sprinkle with the Parmesan cheese and basil.

3. **SERVE** with WHEAT THINS Snack Crackers or vegetables.

VARIATION:
Prepare as directed, substituting KRAFT Balsamic Vinaigrette Dressing for the Italian dressing.

easy layered tomato dip

PREP: 10 min. | **TOTAL:** 3 hours 10 min. | **MAKES:** 3 cups dip or 24 servings, 2 Tbsp. dip and 16 crackers each.

▶ what you need!

1 pkg. (8 oz.) PHILADELPHIA Neufchâtel Cheese, softened

2 cloves garlic, minced

2 small tomatoes, chopped

3 green onions, sliced

¼ cup KRAFT 2% Milk Shredded Cheddar Cheese

WHEAT THINS Reduced Fat Baked Snack Crackers

▶ make it!

1. **MIX** Neufchâtel and garlic until well blended.

2. **SPREAD** onto bottom of shallow serving bowl or 9-inch pie plate; top with tomatoes, onions and Cheddar. Refrigerate 3 hours or until chilled.

3. **SERVE** with crackers.

SUBSTITUTE:
Prepare using WHEAT THINS Multi-Grain Snack Crackers.

nut and honey pear dip

PREP: 5 min. | TOTAL: 7 min. | MAKES: 16 servings, 2 Tbsp. dip and 5 crackers each.

▶ what you need!

½ cup PLANTERS Walnut Pieces

¼ cup honey, divided

1 pkg. (8 oz.) PHILADELPHIA Neufchâtel Cheese, softened

1 medium pear, chopped

RITZ Reduced Fat Crackers

▶ make it!

1. **MIX** walnuts and 2 Tbsp. of the honey in small bowl; set aside.

2. **COMBINE** Neufchâtel, remaining 2 Tbsp. honey and pear in medium bowl until well blended. Spread mixture onto bottom of 9-inch pie plate or bowl. Top with walnut mixture.

3. **MICROWAVE** on HIGH 1 to 2 min. or until heated through. Serve with crackers.

STORAGE KNOW-HOW:
Nuts have a high oil content that makes them susceptible to spoilage. To keep shelled nuts from turning rancid, store them in the refrigerator. If you buy nuts in bulk and want to keep them for several months, store them in the freezer.

peanutty dip

PREP: 5 min. | TOTAL: 5 min. | MAKES: 3 servings, 2 Tbsp. dip, 7 crackers, and ⅓ apple and ⅓ pear each.

▶ what you need!

2 oz. (¼ of 8-oz. pkg.) PHILADELPHIA Neufchâtel Cheese, softened

1 Tbsp. peanut butter

1 Tbsp. honey

1 Tbsp. milk

21 RITZ Sticks Crackers

1 apple, cut into slices

1 pear, cut into slices

▶ make it!

1. **MIX** Neufchâtel, peanut butter, honey and milk in small bowl until well blended.

2. **SERVE** with crackers, apple and pear for dipping.

FUN IDEA:
For an easy dessert, serve with TEDDY GRAHAMS Graham Snacks, HONEY MAID Grahams Honey Sticks or NILLA Wafers.

PHILLY cheesy chili dip

PREP: 5 min. | TOTAL: 6 min. | MAKES: 3 cups or 24 servings, 2 Tbsp. each.

▶ what you need!

1 pkg. (8 oz.) PHILADELPHIA Cream Cheese, softened

1 can (15 oz.) chili

½ cup KRAFT Shredded Cheddar Cheese

2 Tbsp. chopped cilantro

NABISCO Crackers or cut-up fresh vegetables

▶ make it!

1. **SPREAD** cream cheese onto bottom of microwaveable pie plate; top with chili and Cheddar.

2. **MICROWAVE** on HIGH 45 sec. to 1 min. or until Cheddar is melted; sprinkle with cilantro.

3. **SERVE** with assorted NABISCO Crackers or vegetables.

SERVE AS A TOPPER:
Place unwrapped pkg. of cream cheese on microwaveable plate; top with chili and Cheddar. Then, microwave and garnish with cilantro before serving as directed.

NOTE:
Use your favorite variety of canned chili—with or without beans, regular or spicy.

blt dip

PREP: 15 min. | TOTAL: 15 min. | MAKES: 2 cups or 16 servings, 2 Tbsp. each.

▶ what you need!

1 pkg. (8 oz.) PHILADELPHIA Cream Cheese, softened

¾ cup shredded or chopped romaine lettuce

2 plum tomatoes, seeded, chopped

4 slices OSCAR MAYER Bacon, crisply cooked, drained and crumbled

WHEAT THINS Snack Crackers or cut-up fresh vegetables

▶ make it!

1. **SPREAD** cream cheese onto bottom of 9-inch pie plate.

2. **TOP** with lettuce and tomatoes; sprinkle with bacon.

3. **SERVE** with WHEAT THINS Snack Crackers or vegetables.

VARIATION:
Prepare as directed, using PHILADELPHIA Neufchâtel Cheese and LOUIS RICH Turkey Bacon.

Main Event

Casseroles and entrées that are sure to please

tandoori chicken kabobs

PREP: 10 min. | TOTAL: 50 min. | MAKES: 4 servings.

▸ what you need!

2 oz. (¼ of 8-oz. pkg.) PHILADELPHIA Cream Cheese, softened

2 Tbsp. tandoori paste

1 lb. boneless skinless chicken breasts, cut into 2-inch pieces

▸ make it!

1. **MIX** cream cheese and tandoori paste in medium bowl. Add chicken; toss to coat. Refrigerate 30 min. to marinate.

2. **HEAT** broiler. Remove chicken from marinade; reserve marinade. Thread chicken onto 4 skewers; brush with reserved marinade. Place on rack of broiler pan.

3. **BROIL,** 6 inches from heat source, 8 to 10 min. or until chicken is done, turning after 5 min.

NOTE:
If using wooden skewers, soak skewers in water 30 min. before using to assemble kabobs to prevent the skewers from burning on the grill.

SERVING SUGGESTION:
Serve over hot cooked basmati rice and with a mixed green salad.

potato-topped mini meatloaves

PREP: 15 min. | TOTAL: 40 min. | MAKES: 6 servings, 2 meatloaves each.

▶ what you need!

1 lb. ground beef

1 pkg. (6 oz.) STOVE TOP Stuffing Mix

1 cup water

2 Tbsp. A.1. Original Steak Sauce

6 oz. (¾ of 8-oz. pkg.) PHILADELPHIA Cream Cheese, cubed

3 cloves garlic, minced

3 cups hot mashed potatoes

¼ cup chopped fresh parsley

1 jar (12 oz.) beef gravy, warmed

▶ make it!

1. **HEAT** oven to 375°F.

2. **MIX** meat, stuffing mix, water and steak sauce; press into 12 muffin cups sprayed with cooking spray.

3. **BAKE** 20 to 25 min. or until done (160°F).

4. **ADD** cream cheese and garlic to potatoes; stir until cream cheese is melted. Stir in parsley. Scoop over meatloaves. Serve with gravy.

HEALTHY LIVING:
Save 80 calories and 10 grams of fat including 4 grams of saturated fat per serving, by preparing with extra-lean beef, PHILADELPHIA Neufchâtel Cheese and fat-free beef gravy.

SERVING SUGGESTION:
Serve with a mixed green salad and glass of fat-free milk to round out the meal!

shrimp pizza squares

PREP: 10 min. | TOTAL: 35 min. | MAKES: 36 servings.

▶ what you need!

1 can (13.8 oz.) refrigerated pizza crust

1 lb. uncooked deveined peeled medium shrimp

3 cloves garlic, minced

2 Tbsp. KRAFT Zesty Italian Dressing

4 oz. (½ of 8-oz. pkg.) PHILADELPHIA Cream Cheese, softened

1 cup KRAFT Shredded Italian Mozzarella-Parmesan Cheese Blend*

1 cup roasted red pepper strips

¼ cup chopped fresh basil

*Made with quality cheeses crafted in the USA.

▶ make it!

1. **HEAT** oven to 425°F.

2. **UNROLL** dough onto baking sheet sprayed lightly with cooking spray; press into 13×9-inch rectangle. Bake 12 to 15 min. or until lightly browned.

3. **MEANWHILE,** cook shrimp and garlic in dressing in large skillet on medium-high heat 3 to 5 min. or until shrimp turn pink, stirring frequently. Remove from heat; drain.

4. **SPREAD** cream cheese onto pizza crust, leaving ¼-inch border around sides. Top with shrimp, shredded cheese and peppers. Bake 10 min. or until shredded cheese is melted. Sprinkle with basil.

SUBSTITUTE:
For variety, top pizza with sliced fresh mushrooms and/or chopped artichoke hearts instead of the roasted peppers.

SPECIAL EXTRA:
Sprinkle pizza with ½ tsp. crushed red pepper, or more to taste, before baking as directed.

tuscan chicken simmer

PREP: 5 min. | TOTAL: 25 min. | MAKES: 4 servings.

▶ what you need!

4 small boneless skinless chicken breast halves (1 lb.)

4 oz. (½ of 8-oz. pkg.) PHILADELPHIA Cream Cheese, cubed

¼ cup water

¼ cup pesto

2 cups grape or cherry tomatoes

1 cup KRAFT Finely Shredded Italian Five Cheese Blend*

Made with quality cheeses crafted in the USA.

▶ make it!

1. **HEAT** large nonstick skillet sprayed with cooking spray on medium-high heat. Add chicken; cover skillet with lid. Cook 5 to 7 min. on each side or until chicken is cooked through (165°F). Remove chicken from skillet; keep warm.

2. **REDUCE** heat to medium. Add cream cheese, water, pesto and tomatoes to skillet. Cook, uncovered, 2 min. or until heated through, stirring occasionally.

3. **RETURN** chicken to skillet. Cook and stir 1 min. or until chicken is coated and heated through. Sprinkle with shredded cheese.

SERVING SUGGESTION:
Serve with hot cooked spinach fettuccine or ravioli.

roast pork tenderloin supper

PREP: 15 min. | TOTAL: 45 min. | MAKES: 6 servings.

▶ what you need!

2 pork tenderloins (1½ lb.)

¼ cup GREY POUPON Dijon Mustard

2 tsp. dried thyme leaves

1 pkg. (6 oz.) STOVE TOP Stuffing Mix for Chicken

½ cup fat-free reduced-sodium chicken broth

4 oz. (½ of 8-oz. pkg.) PHILADELPHIA Neufchâtel Cheese, cubed

1 lb. fresh green beans (about 3 cups), steamed

▶ make it!

1. **HEAT** oven to 400°F. Heat large nonstick skillet on medium heat. Add meat; cook 5 min. or until browned on all sides, turning occasionally. Remove meat from skillet, reserving meat drippings in skillet. Place meat in 13×9-inch baking dish. Combine mustard and thyme; spread evenly onto meat.

2. **BAKE** 20 to 25 min. or until cooked through (160°F). Transfer to carving board; tent with foil. Let stand 5 min. Meanwhile, prepare stuffing as directed on pkg., reducing the spread to 1 Tbsp.

3. **ADD** broth to same skillet. Bring to boil on high heat. Reduce heat to medium-low. Add Neufchâtel; cook 2 min. or until Neufchâtel is completely melted and mixture is well blended, stirring constantly.

4. **CUT** meat into thin slices. Serve topped with the cream cheese sauce along with the stuffing and beans.

NOTE:
If you purchased the broth in a 32-oz. pkg., store remaining broth in refrigerator up to 1 week. Or if you purchased a 14-oz. can, pour the remaining broth into a glass container; cover and store in refrigerator up to 1 week.

NUTRITION BONUS:
This oh-so-easy, low-calorie dinner features foods from 3 different food groups, helping you to eat a variety of foods.

fish in roasted red pepper sauce

PREP: 10 min. | TOTAL: 30 min. | MAKES: 4 servings.

▶ what you need!

1 lb. cod fillets (4 fillets)

¼ cup flour

¼ cup KRAFT Zesty Italian Dressing

½ cup sliced onions

2 oz. (¼ of 8-oz. pkg.) PHILADELPHIA Cream Cheese, softened

¼ cup roasted red peppers

¼ cup chicken broth

1 clove garlic, peeled

2 Tbsp. chopped cilantro

▶ make it!

1. **COAT** both sides of fish with flour; set aside. Heat dressing in large skillet on medium-high heat. Add onions; cook and stir until crisp-tender. Add fish; cook 5 to 7 min. on each side or until fish flakes easily with fork.

2. **MEANWHILE,** place cream cheese, red peppers, broth and garlic in blender container; cover. Blend until smooth. Spoon into medium saucepan. Bring to boil on medium-high heat. Reduce heat to low; simmer 5 min., stirring occasionally.

3. **PLACE** fish on serving platter; top with the cream cheese mixture. Sprinkle with cilantro.

MAKE IT EASY:
Substitute jarred roasted red peppers for the roasted fresh red peppers.

SPECIAL EXTRA:
Prepare as directed, using roasted poblano peppers.

BUYING AND STORING FROZEN FISH & SHELLFISH:
When purchasing frozen fish or shellfish, make sure it is well wrapped and solidly frozen, with no odor. Always check the "sell-by" date on the pkg. Store it in the refrigerator, tightly wrapped, for up to 2 days. Never refreeze fish or shellfish once it's been thawed.

creamy thai green curry chicken & rice

PREP: 15 min. | TOTAL: 30 min. | MAKES: 4 servings, 2 cups each.

▶ what you need!

1 Tbsp. canola oil

2 Tbsp. green curry paste

1 lb. boneless skinless chicken breasts, cut into bite-size pieces

1 small onion, thinly sliced

1 each red and green bell pepper, cut into thin strips, then cut crosswise in half

4 oz. (½ of 8-oz. pkg.) PHILADELPHIA Cream Cheese, cubed

¼ cup milk

⅛ tsp. white pepper

4 cups hot cooked long-grain white rice

▶ make it!

1. **HEAT** oil in large nonstick skillet on medium heat. Stir in curry paste until well blended. Add chicken and onions; cook and stir 6 to 8 min. or until chicken is done (165°F). Stir in peppers; cook 4 to 5 min. or until crisp-tender.

2. **ADD** cream cheese, milk and white pepper; cook until cream cheese is melted and evenly coats chicken and vegetables, stirring frequently.

3. **SERVE** over rice.

SUBSTITUTE:
Prepare using red curry paste.

KEEPING IT SAFE:
When thawing frozen chicken, place in refrigerator, allowing about 5 hours per pound of chicken. Never thaw chicken at room temperature due to the risk of bacterial growth.

family-favorite roast chicken

PREP: 10 min. | TOTAL: 1 hour 40 min. | MAKES: 8 servings.

▶ what you need!

1 (4½-lb.) roasting chicken

¼ tsp. black pepper

⅛ tsp. salt

1 medium lemon, washed

4 oz. (½ of 8-oz. pkg.) PHILADELPHIA Cream Cheese, softened

1 Tbsp. Italian seasoning

½ cup KRAFT Zesty Italian Dressing

▶ make it!

1. **HEAT** oven to 350°F. Rinse chicken; pat dry with paper towel. Use the tip of a sharp knife to separate the chicken skin from the meat in the chicken breast and tops of the legs. Sprinkle chicken both inside and out with the pepper and salt. Place in 13×9-inch baking dish.

2. **GRATE** the lemon; mix the peel with cream cheese and Italian seasoning. Use a small spoon or your fingers to carefully stuff the cream cheese mixture under the chicken skin, pushing the cream cheese mixture carefully toward the legs, being careful to not tear the skin.

3. **CUT** the lemon in half; squeeze both halves into small bowl. Add dressing; beat with wire whisk until well blended. Drizzle evenly over chicken. Place the squeezed lemon halves inside the chicken cavity. Insert an ovenproof meat thermometer into thickest part of 1 of the chicken's thighs.

4. **BAKE** 1 hour 30 min. or until chicken is no longer pink in center (165°F), basting occasionally with the pan juices.

creamy bow-tie pasta with chicken and broccoli

PREP: 10 min | TOTAL: 25 min | MAKES: 6 servings, about 1½ cups each

▶ what you need!

3 cups (8 oz.) farfalle (bow-tie pasta), uncooked

4 cups broccoli florets

3 Tbsp. KRAFT Roasted Red Pepper Italian with Parmesan Dressing

6 small boneless skinless chicken breast halves (1½ lb.)

2 cloves garlic, minced

2 cups tomato-basil spaghetti sauce

4 oz. (½ of 8-oz. pkg.) PHILADELPHIA Neufchâtel Cheese, cubed

¼ cup KRAFT 100% Grated Parmesan Cheese

▶ make it!

1. **COOK** pasta as directed on pkg., adding broccoli to the cooking water for the last 3 min. of the pasta cooking time. Meanwhile, heat dressing in large nonstick skillet on medium heat. Add chicken and garlic; cook 5 min. Turn chicken over; continue cooking 4 to 5 min. or until chicken is cooked through (165°F).

2. **DRAIN** pasta mixture in colander; return to pan and set aside. Add spaghetti sauce and Neufchâtel cheese to chicken in skillet; cook on medium-low heat 2 to 3 min. or until Neufchâtel cheese is completely melted, mixture is well blended and chicken is coated with sauce, stirring occasionally. Remove chicken from skillet; keep warm. Add sauce mixture to pasta mixture; mix well. Transfer to 6 serving bowls.

3. **CUT** chicken crosswise into thick slices; fan out chicken over pasta mixture. Sprinkle evenly with Parmesan cheese.

SUBSTITUTE:
Prepare as directed, using whole wheat or multi-grain pasta.

seafood enchiladas

▶ what you need!

½ lb. cleaned shrimp, chopped

1 can (6 oz.) crabmeat, drained, flaked

1 can (7 oz.) whole kernel corn, drained

½ cup chopped green onions (about 2)

½ tsp. ground red pepper (cayenne), divided

1 pkg. (8 oz.) KRAFT 2% Milk Shredded Cheddar Cheese, divided

10 flour tortillas (7 inch)

4 oz. (½ of 8-oz. pkg.) PHILADELPHIA Cream Cheese, cubed

¾ cup milk

▶ make it!

1. **HEAT** oven to 350°F. Cook and stir shrimp in medium nonstick skillet sprayed with cooking spray on medium heat 2 min. Add crabmeat, corn, onions and ¼ tsp. of the pepper; mix well. Cook and stir an additional 2 min. or until shrimp turn pink. Remove from heat. Stir in 1 cup of the shredded cheese.

2. **SPOON** ⅓ cup of the seafood mixture onto each tortilla; roll up. Place, seam-sides down, in lightly greased 13×9-inch baking dish. Place cream cheese in medium saucepan. Add milk; cook on medium-low heat 5 min. or until cream cheese is completely melted and mixture is well blended, stirring frequently. Pour evenly over enchiladas.

3. **BAKE** 5 min. Remove from oven. Sprinkle with remaining shredded cheese. Bake an additional 5 min. or until cheese is melted. Sprinkle with remaining ¼ tsp. pepper.

chicken & pepper pasta bake

PREP: 25 min. | TOTAL: 45 min. | MAKES: 4 servings, 2 cups each.

▶ what you need!

3 cups rigatoni, uncooked

1 lb. boneless skinless chicken breasts, cut into bite-size pieces

1 each large red and green bell pepper, coarsely chopped

1 jar (24 oz.) spaghetti sauce

2 oz. (¼ of 8-oz. pkg.) PHILADELPHIA Cream Cheese, cubed

1 cup KRAFT Shredded Mozzarella Cheese

¼ cup KRAFT Grated Parmesan Cheese

▶ make it!

1. **HEAT** oven to 375°F.

2. **COOK** pasta as directed on pkg. Meanwhile, heat large nonstick skillet on medium-high heat. Add chicken; cook and stir 2 min. Add peppers; cook and stir 3 min. Stir in spaghetti sauce; simmer 6 to 8 min. or until chicken is done and peppers are crisp-tender, stirring occasionally. Add cream cheese; cook and stir 1 to 2 min. or until melted.

3. **DRAIN** pasta. Add to chicken mixture; toss to coat. Spoon half into 8- or 9-inch square baking dish. Top with ½ cup mozzarella and 2 Tbsp. Parmesan. Repeat layers.

4. **BAKE** 20 min. or until heated through.

SPECIAL EXTRA:
Garnish with chopped fresh basil or parsley just before serving.

enchiladas suizas

► what you need!

1 pkg. (8 oz.) PHILADELPHIA Cream Cheese, softened, divided

½ cup sliced green onions

1 cup KRAFT Shredded Sharp Cheddar Cheese

1 cup KRAFT Shredded Monterey Jack Cheese

2 cans (4 oz. each) chopped green chilies, drained

½ tsp. ground cumin

3 eggs

1 Tbsp. oil

12 corn tortillas

2 jars (8 oz. each) enchilada sauce

1 can (4¼ oz.) sliced black olives, drained

► make it!

1. **HEAT** oven to 350°F. Place half of the cream cheese and the onions in small bowl. Beat with electric mixer on medium speed until well blended; set aside for later use.

2. **PLACE** remaining cream cheese, the Cheddar cheese, Monterey Jack cheese, green chilies and cumin in large bowl. Beat with electric mixer on medium speed until well blended. Add eggs, 1 at a time, beating well after each addition; set aside. Heat oil in medium skillet. Add tortillas; cook just until warmed. Spoon 2 Tbsp. of the cheese mixture onto each tortilla; roll up. Place, seam-sides down, in 13×9-inch baking dish; top with the enchilada sauce.

3. **BAKE** 20 min. or until heated through. Top with the reserved cream cheese mixture and the olives.

SERVING SUGGESTION:
Serve with a mixed green salad for added color and texture.

SUBSTITUTE:
Substitute PHILADELPHIA Neufchâtel Cheese for the cream cheese.

bacon 'n eggs pie

PREP: 20 min. | TOTAL: 32 min. | MAKES: 6 servings.

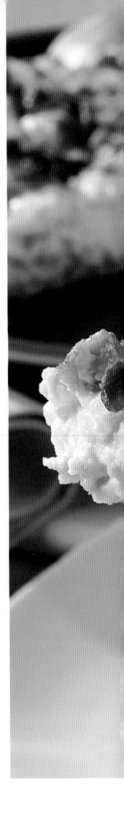

▶ what you need!

1 can (7.5 oz.) refrigerated buttermilk biscuits

2 Tbsp. butter or margarine

6 eggs

⅓ cup milk

¼ tsp. each salt and black pepper

3 oz. PHILADELPHIA Cream Cheese, cubed

6 slices OSCAR MAYER Bacon, cooked, crumbled

▶ make it!

1. **HEAT** oven to 375°F.

2. **SEPARATE** biscuits. Place on bottom and up side of 9-inch pie plate; press together to form crust. Bake 10 to 12 min. or until lightly browned.

3. **MEANWHILE,** melt butter in medium skillet on low heat. Whisk eggs, milk and seasonings until well blended; pour into skillet. Cook until eggs begin to set, stirring occasionally. Add cream cheese; cook until cream cheese is melted and eggs are set, stirring occasionally.

4. **SPOON** egg mixture into crust; top with bacon.

SERVING SUGGESTION:
For a delightful brunch idea, serve with a seasonal fresh fruit salad.

SPECIAL EXTRA:
Garnish with chopped fresh parsley just before serving.

diner special meatloaf

PREP: 15 min. | **TOTAL:** 1 hour 15 min. | **MAKES:** 4 servings.

▶ what you need!

- 1 lb. lean ground beef
- ½ cup KRAFT Original Barbecue Sauce
- ½ cup dry bread crumbs
- 1 egg, lightly beaten
- 1¼ cups water
- ¾ cup milk
- 2 Tbsp. butter or margarine
- ½ tsp. salt
- 1½ cups instant potato flakes
- 3 oz. PHILADELPHIA Cream Cheese, cubed
- 2 KRAFT Singles

▶ make it!

1. **HEAT** oven to 375°F. Mix meat, barbecue sauce, bread crumbs and egg. Shape into loaf in 12×8-inch baking dish.

2. **BAKE** 55 min. Meanwhile, bring water to boil in medium saucepan. Add milk, butter and salt; stir in potato flakes. Add cream cheese; stir until completely melted.

3. **SPREAD** potato mixture over meatloaf; top with Singles. Bake an additional 5 min. or until Singles begin to melt.

ROUND OUT THE MEAL:
Serve with a steamed green vegetable, such as green beans, and a whole wheat roll.

GREAT SUBSTITUTE:
Substitute 1 pkg. (16 oz.) frozen LOUIS RICH Ground Turkey for the ground beef.

SPECIAL EXTRA:
Garnish with chopped fresh chives just before serving.

linguine with silky mushroom sauce

PREP: 5 min. | TOTAL: 20 min. | MAKES: 4 servings.

▶ what you need!

- ½ lb. linguine, uncooked
- 1 pkg. (½ lb.) sliced fresh mushrooms
- ½ cup chicken broth
- ½ cup (½ of 8-oz. tub) PHILADELPHIA Chive & Onion Light Cream Cheese Spread
- 2 cups baby spinach leaves
- Black pepper

▶ make it!

1. **COOK** pasta as directed on pkg.

2. **MEANWHILE,** heat skillet sprayed with cooking spray on medium-high heat. Add mushrooms; cook and stir 8 min. or until lightly browned. Add broth and cream cheese spread; mix well. Add spinach; cook just until wilted.

3. **DRAIN** pasta; toss with sauce. Sprinkle with black pepper.

SPECIAL EXTRA:
Try a sprinkle of KRAFT Grated Parmesan over this dish before serving.

zesty chicken pot pie

PREP: 20 min. | TOTAL: 45 min. | MAKES: 8 servings.

▶ what you need!

12 oz. (1½ pkg. [8 oz. each]) PHILADELPHIA Cream Cheese, cubed

½ cup chicken broth

3 cups chopped cooked chicken

2 pkg. (10 oz. each) frozen mixed vegetables, thawed

1 env. GOOD SEASONS Italian Salad Dressing & Recipe Mix

1 ready-to-use refrigerated pie crust (½ of 15-oz. pkg.)

▶ make it!

1. **HEAT** oven to 425°F. Place cream cheese in large saucepan. Add broth; cook on low heat until cream cheese is completely melted, stirring frequently with wire whisk. Stir in chicken, vegetables and salad dressing mix.

2. **SPOON** into 9-inch pie plate. Cover with pie crust; seal and flute edge. Cut several slits in crust to allow steam to escape. Place pie plate on baking sheet.

3. **BAKE** 20 to 25 min. or until golden brown.

SERVING SUGGESTION:
Serve with a mixed green salad and glass of fat-free milk.

MAKE AHEAD:
Prepare as directed except for baking. Wrap securely; freeze. When ready to bake, unwrap. Place strips of foil around edge to prevent overbrowning. Bake frozen pie at 425°F for 1 hour and 10 min. or until heated through.

SUBSTITUTES:
Prepare as directed, using PHILADELPHIA Neufchâtel Cheese, GOOD SEASONS Zesty Italian Dressing or substituting turkey for the chicken.

white & gold pizza

PREP: 10 min. | TOTAL: 43 min. | MAKES: 6 servings.

▶ what you need!

3 Tbsp. olive oil, divided

1 large sweet onion, thinly sliced

1 lb. frozen pizza dough, thawed

1 large clove garlic, minced

4 oz. (½ of 8-oz. pkg.) PHILADELPHIA Cream Cheese, softened

¾ cup KRAFT Shredded Mozzarella Cheese

½ cup DIGIORNO® Grated Romano Cheese*

½ tsp. crushed red pepper

DIGIORNO® is a registered trademark of Nestlé, used under license.

▶ make it!

1. **HEAT** oven to 425°F.

2. **HEAT** 1 Tbsp. oil in large skillet on medium heat. Add onions; cook 15 to 20 min. or until tender and golden brown, stirring occasionally.

3. **MEANWHILE,** place pizza dough on lightly floured baking sheet; pat to 16×12-inch rectangle. Mix garlic and remaining oil; spread onto dough. Bake 10 min.

4. **SPREAD** cream cheese onto crust; top with remaining cheeses, onions and crushed red pepper. Bake 10 to 12 min. or until crust is golden brown.

MAKE AHEAD:
Caramelized onions can be made ahead of time. Cool, then refrigerate up to 2 days before using as directed.

SMOKED SALMON & CAPERS PIZZA:
Prepare as directed, using PHILADELPHIA Salmon Cream Cheese Spread and substituting 2 tsp. capers for the crushed red pepper.

SERVING SUGGESTION:
For added color and texture, serve with a mixed green salad tossed with your favorite KRAFT Light Dressing.

puffy french toast casserole

PREP: 10 min. | TOTAL: 8 hours 55 min. | MAKES: 12 servings.

▶ what you need!

1 loaf (8 oz.) French bread, cut into ½-inch cubes (about 6 cups)

1½ pkg. (8 oz. each) PHILADELPHIA Cream Cheese, cubed

8 eggs

2 cups milk

½ cup maple-flavored or pancake syrup

½ cup PLANTERS Pecan Pieces

▶ make it!

1. **PLACE** bread cubes in greased 13×9-inch baking dish; top evenly with the cream cheese.

2. **BEAT** eggs, milk and syrup with wire whisk until well blended. Pour over ingredients in baking dish; cover. Refrigerate overnight.

3. **HEAT** oven to 375°F. Bake, uncovered, 35 min.; sprinkle with the pecans. Bake an additional 10 min. or until center is set. Serve with additional syrup, if desired.

FAMILY FUN:
This is a great breakfast-time casserole when you have family or friends visiting from out of town. It goes together quickly the night before so that you can spend more time with your guests!

ROUND OUT THE MEAL:
For a delightful brunch idea, serve this casserole with a seasonal fresh fruit salad.

Sensational Sides

Breads, vegetable bakes, soups, and other accompaniments

chive & onion mashed potatoes

PREP: 10 min. | TOTAL: 35 min. | MAKES: 10 servings, ½ cup each.

▶ what you need!

2 lb. potatoes, peeled, quartered (about 6 cups)

½ cup milk

1 tub (8 oz.) PHILADELPHIA Chive & Onion Cream Cheese Spread

¼ cup KRAFT Ranch Dressing

▶ make it!

1. **PLACE** potatoes and enough water to cover in 3-qt. saucepan. Bring to boil.

2. **REDUCE** heat to medium; cook 20 to 25 min. or until tender. Drain.

3. **MASH** potatoes, gradually stirring in milk, cream cheese spread and dressing until light and fluffy. Serve immediately.

MAKE AHEAD:
Mix ingredients as directed; spoon into 1½-qt. casserole dish. Cover. Refrigerate several hours or overnight. When ready to serve, bake, uncovered, at 350°F 1 hour or until heated through.

SUBSTITUTE:
Substitute KRAFT Three Cheese Ranch Dressing for Ranch Dressing.

creamed corn

PREP: 5 min. | TOTAL: 10 min. | MAKES: 6 servings, ½ cup each.

▶ what you need!

2 oz. (¼ of 8-oz. pkg.) PHILADELPHIA Cream Cheese, cubed

2 Tbsp. milk

1 can (14¾ oz.) cream-style corn

1 pkg. (10 oz.) frozen corn, thawed

½ cup KRAFT Shredded Sharp Cheddar Cheese

⅓ cup sliced green onions

▶ make it!

1. **COOK** cream cheese and milk in medium saucepan on medium heat until cream cheese is melted, stirring frequently.

2. **STIR** in corns; cook 4 min. or until heated through, stirring occasionally.

3. **SPOON** into serving dish; sprinkle with Cheddar and onions.

SPECIAL EXTRA:
Stir in a dash or two of hot pepper sauce.

creamy sweet whipped carrots

`PREP: 15 min. | TOTAL: 15 min. | MAKES: 4 servings.`

▶ what you need!

1 lb. baby carrots

4 oz. (½ of 8-oz. pkg.) PHILADELPHIA Fat Free Cream Cheese

2 Tbsp. fat-free milk

2 Tbsp. brown sugar, divided

¼ tsp. ground cinnamon

▶ make it!

1. **PLACE** carrots in 1½-qt. microwaveable bowl or casserole dish. Add enough water to completely cover carrots. Microwave on HIGH 10 min. or until carrots are tender; drain.

2. **PLACE** carrots in food processor container. Add cream cheese, milk and 1 Tbsp. of the sugar; cover. Process until well blended. Place in serving bowl.

3. **MIX** remaining 1 Tbsp. sugar and cinnamon; sprinkle over carrot mixture.

USE YOUR STOVE:
Place carrots in saucepan. Add enough water to cover. Bring to boil on high heat. Reduce heat to medium-low; cover. Simmer 20 min. or until carrots are tender; drain. Continue as directed.

TAKE A SHORTCUT:
Substitute 1 lb. frozen carrot slices for baby carrots. Heat as directed on pkg. Continue as directed.

honey cream filled crescents

PREP: 10 min. | TOTAL: 24 min. | MAKES: 8 servings, 1 crescent each.

▶ what you need!

4 oz. (½ of 8-oz. pkg.) PHILADELPHIA Cream Cheese, softened

3 Tbsp. honey, divided

¼ cup PLANTERS Sliced Almonds

1 pkg. (8 oz.) refrigerated crescent dinner rolls

Dash ground cinnamon

▶ make it!

1. **HEAT** oven to 375°F. Mix cream cheese and 2 Tbsp. of the honey. Stir in almonds.

2. **UNROLL** crescent roll dough; separate into 8 triangles. Spread 1 rounded Tbsp. cream cheese mixture onto each triangle; roll up each loosely, starting at shortest side of triangle, rolling to opposite point. Place rolls on ungreased baking sheet; curve each into crescent shape. Sprinkle with cinnamon.

3. **BAKE** 12 to 14 min. or until golden brown. Serve rolls warm, drizzled with remaining honey.

SIZE IT UP:
Enjoy 1 serving of this crescent roll filled with a sweet treat when you entertain friends.

GREAT SUBSTITUTE:
Substitute PLANTERS Chopped Pecans for almonds.

crispy-topped creamy spinach

PREP: 10 min. | TOTAL: 35 min. | MAKES: 12 servings.

▸ what you need!

2 pkg. (10 oz. each) frozen chopped spinach, thawed, well drained

1 tub (8 oz.) PHILADELPHIA Chive & Onion Cream Cheese Spread

½ cup KRAFT Ranch Dressing

2 eggs, lightly beaten

1½ cups KRAFT Shredded Cheddar Cheese, divided

1 cup crushed RITZ Crackers, divided

▸ make it!

1. **HEAT** oven to 375°F. Mix spinach, cream cheese spread, dressing, eggs and ¾ cup of the Cheddar cheese in large bowl. Stir in ½ cup of the crushed crackers.

2. **SPOON** spinach mixture evenly into greased 2-qt. ovenproof casserole dish. Sprinkle with remaining ½ cup crushed crackers and remaining ¾ cup Cheddar cheese.

3. **BAKE** 20 to 25 min. or until heated through and cheese on top is melted.

HEALTHY LIVING:
Counting calories? Save 50 calories and 8 grams of fat per serving by using PHILADELPHIA Chive & Onion Light Cream Cheese Spread, KRAFT Light Ranch Dressing, KRAFT 2% Milk Shredded Reduced Fat Cheddar Cheese and RITZ Reduced Fat Crackers.

HOW TO THAW FROZEN SPINACH:
Thaw frozen spinach in refrigerator overnight or unwrap; place in microwaveable bowl and thaw in microwave as directed on pkg. Be sure to squeeze well after thawing to remove as much water as possible.

mashed potato layer bake

PREP: 25 min. | TOTAL: 45 min. | MAKES: 14 servings, ½ cup each.

▶ what you need!

4 large white potatoes, peeled, chopped and cooked

2 large sweet potatoes, peeled, chopped and cooked

1 tub (8 oz.) PHILADELPHIA Chive & Onion Cream Cheese Spread, divided

½ cup BREAKSTONE'S or KNUDSEN Sour Cream, divided

¼ tsp. each salt and black pepper

¼ cup KRAFT Shredded or 100% Grated Parmesan Cheese, divided

¼ cup KRAFT Shredded Cheddar Cheese, divided

▶ make it!

1. **HEAT** oven to 375°F. Place potatoes in separate bowls. Add half each of the cream cheese and sour cream to each bowl; season with salt and pepper. Mash with potato masher or fork until creamy.

2. **STIR** half of the Parmesan cheese into white potatoes. Stir half of the Cheddar cheese into sweet potatoes. Alternately layer half each of the white potato and sweet potato mixture in 2-qt. clear glass casserole. Repeat layers.

3. **BAKE** 15 min. Sprinkle with remaining cheeses; bake 5 more min. or until cheeses are melted.

MAKE AHEAD:
Assemble casserole as directed. Do not add the cheese topping. Cover and refrigerate casserole and cheese topping separately up to 3 days. When ready to serve, uncover and bake casserole as directed, increasing baking time as needed until casserole is heated through. Top with remaining cheeses and continue as directed.

AHA!:
This recipe combines everyone's favorite potatoes into 1 bowl—no need to make 2 different kinds of potatoes! It also makes a usually plain dish tasty and beautiful.

mini new potato bites

PREP: 20 min. | TOTAL: 1 hour 20 min. | MAKES: 15 servings, 2 topped potato halves each.

▶ what you need!

1½ lb. new potatoes (about 15 potatoes)

4 oz. (½ of 8-oz. pkg.) PHILADELPHIA Cream Cheese, softened

2 Tbsp. BREAKSTONE'S or KNUDSEN Sour Cream

2 Tbsp. KRAFT 100% Grated Parmesan Cheese

4 slices OSCAR MAYER Bacon, cooked, crumbled

2 Tbsp. snipped fresh chives

▶ make it!

1. **PLACE** potatoes in large saucepan; add enough water to cover. Bring to boil. Reduce heat to medium-low; cook 15 min. or until potatoes are tender.

2. **MIX** cream cheese, sour cream and Parmesan cheese; cover. Refrigerate until ready to use.

3. **DRAIN** potatoes. Cool slightly. Cut potatoes in half; cut small piece from bottom of each potato half so potato lies flat. Place on serving platter. Top each potato half with 1 tsp. of the cream cheese mixture. Sprinkle with bacon and chives.

MAKE AHEAD:
These potatoes are delicious served hot or cold.

SUBSTITUTION:
Substitute PHILADELPHIA Chive & Onion Cream Cheese Spread for the regular cream cheese for added flavor.

new potatoes in dill cream sauce

PREP: 10 min. | TOTAL: 30 min. | MAKES: 16 servings, about ½ cup each.

▸ what you need!

2½ lb. new red potatoes, quartered

1 tub (8 oz.) PHILADELPHIA Chive & Onion Cream Cheese Spread

¼ cup milk

1 green bell pepper, chopped

3 Tbsp. chopped fresh dill

▸ make it!

1. **PLACE** potatoes in large saucepan. Add enough water to cover potatoes. Bring to boil on medium-high heat. Reduce heat to medium; simmer 15 min. or until potatoes are tender. Drain.

2. **MEANWHILE,** mix cream cheese spread, milk and peppers in large microwaveable bowl. Microwave on HIGH 40 to 50 sec. or until cream cheese spread is melted; stir until well blended. Stir in dill.

3. **ADD** potatoes; toss to coat.

SUBSTITUTE:
Substitute chopped fresh basil leaves or 2 tsp. dill weed for the chopped fresh dill.

CREATIVE LEFTOVERS:
Cover and refrigerate any leftovers. Serve as a cold potato salad, stirring in a small amount of additional milk to thin, if necessary.

BEST OF SEASON:
New potatoes make a great addition to any spring meal. Their smaller size helps them to cook more quickly than regular potatoes.

twice-baked sweet potatoes

PREP: 10 min. | TOTAL: 53 min. | MAKES: 4 servings.

▶ what you need!

2 large sweet potatoes (1½ lb.)

2 oz. (¼ of 8-oz. pkg.) PHILADELPHIA Neufchâtel Cheese, cubed

2 Tbsp. fat-free milk

1 Tbsp. brown sugar

¼ tsp. ground cinnamon

¼ cup PLANTERS Pecan Pieces

▶ make it!

1. **HEAT** oven to 425°F.

2. **CUT** potatoes lengthwise in half; place, cut-sides down, in foil-lined 15×10×1-inch pan. Bake 30 to 35 min. or until tender.

3. **SCOOP** out centers of potatoes into bowl, leaving ¼-inch-thick shells. Add Neufchâtel, milk, sugar and cinnamon to potatoes; mash until blended.

4. **FILL** shells with potato mixture; top with nuts. Bake 8 min. or until potatoes are heated through and nuts are toasted.

SHORTCUT:
Pierce whole sweet potatoes with fork; wrap in damp paper towels. Microwave on HIGH 7 to 8 min. or until tender. Cut potatoes in half; scoop out centers and continue as directed.

MAKE AHEAD:
Stuff potato shells as directed; refrigerate up to 1 hour. When ready to serve, bake as directed, increasing baking time as needed until filling is heated through.

NUTRITION BONUS:
This classic side gets a twist by using sweet potatoes. Not only are the sweet potatoes rich in vitamin A, but they're also a good source of fiber.

potato leek soup

PREP: 20 min. | TOTAL: 1 hour | MAKES: 8 servings, 1 cup each.

▶ what you need!

2 Tbsp. olive oil

4 large leeks, cut into ¼-inch-thick slices (about 2 lb.)

4 large russet potatoes, peeled, cubed (about 4 cups)

1¼ qt. (5 cups) water

1 tsp. salt

½ tsp. black pepper

1 pkg. (8 oz.) PHILADELPHIA Cream Cheese, cubed

½ cup milk

¼ cup chopped fresh chives

▶ make it!

1. **HEAT** oil in large stockpot on medium heat. Add leeks; cook 5 min. or until tender, stirring occasionally. Add potatoes, water, salt and pepper; cover. Bring to boil; simmer on medium-low 15 to 20 min. or until potatoes are tender. Cool 10 min.

2. **ADD** leek mixture, in batches, to blender; blend until puréed. Return to stockpot. Whisk in cream cheese, a few cubes at a time; cook on medium heat until cream cheese is completely melted, stirring constantly.

3. **ADD** milk; cook until heated through, stirring occasionally. Sprinkle with chives. Serve with PREMIUM Multigrain Saltine Crackers.

JAZZ IT UP:
Sprinkle with black pepper just before serving.

PREPARING LEEKS:
Leeks are grown in sandy soil and must be washed well before using. To prepare leeks, trim the roots and remove the dark green portions. Only the white portion of the leek is used. Chop or slice the white sections, then rinse in water to remove any soil or sand.

HOW TO CLEAN THE BLENDER:
To quickly and easily clean your blender, fill the blender container half full with warm water. Add a few drops of liquid dish soap, then cover tightly. Turn the blender on high speed for 30 sec. Most of the food residue will pour out with the water. Rinse the blender container well, then recheck. If necessary, repeat the process or spot clean.

creamy veggies

PREP: 5 min. | TOTAL: 18 min. | MAKES: 5 servings.

▸ what you need!

1 pkg. (16 oz.) frozen mixed vegetables (California mix)

¼ lb. (4 oz.) VELVEETA 2% Milk Pasteurized Prepared Cheese Product, cut into ½-inch cubes

4 oz. (½ of 8-oz. pkg.) PHILADELPHIA Fat Free Cream Cheese, cubed

▸ make it!

1. **LAYER** ingredients in 1½-qt. microwaveable dish; cover with waxed paper.

2. **MICROWAVE** on HIGH 13 min. or until heated through, turning dish after 7 min.

3. **STIR** until well blended.

USE YOUR OVEN:
Layer ingredients in 1½-qt. casserole. Bake at 350°F for 55 min. or until heated through. Stir until well blended.

NUTRITION BONUS:
This low-fat side dish is a delicious way to eat your vegetables. Not only are the vegetables a good source of both vitamins A and C, but the cheese also provides calcium.

creamy broccoli soup

PREP: 15 min. | TOTAL: 30 min. | MAKES: 6 servings, ¾ cup each.

▶ what you need!

¼ cup chopped onion

1 Tbsp. butter or margarine

1 Tbsp. flour

2 cups milk

4 oz. (½ of 8-oz. pkg.) PHILADELPHIA Cream Cheese, cubed

½ lb. (8 oz.) VELVEETA Pasteurized Prepared Cheese Product, cut into ½-inch cubes

1 pkg. (10 oz.) frozen chopped broccoli, cooked, drained

¼ tsp. ground nutmeg

⅛ tsp. black pepper

▶ make it!

1. **COOK** and stir onions in butter in 2-qt. saucepan on medium-high heat until onions are crisp-tender. Blend in flour.

2. **ADD** milk and cream cheese; cook on medium heat until cream cheese is melted, stirring frequently.

3. **STIR** in remaining ingredients; cook until heated through, stirring occasionally.

SUBSTITUTE:
Prepare using VELVEETA 2% Milk Pasteurized Prepared Cheese Product.

SUBSTITUTE:
Substitute frozen chopped spinach; frozen cauliflower florets, chopped; or frozen asparagus spears, chopped; for the broccoli.

USE YOUR MICROWAVE:
Microwave onions and butter in 2-qt. microwaveable bowl on HIGH 30 sec. or until onions are tender. Stir in milk. Microwave 3 to 4 min. or until heated through, stirring every 2 min. Stir in cream cheese. Microwave 4 to 6 min. or until cream cheese is melted, stirring every 2 min. Stir in remaining ingredients. Microwave 30 sec. or until heated through.

creamy corn and turkey soup

PREP: 10 min. | **TOTAL:** 25 min. | **MAKES:** 6 servings, 1 cup each.

▶ what you need!

½ cup chopped onion

1 cup chopped red bell pepper, divided

2 Tbsp. butter or margarine

4 oz. (½ of 8-oz. pkg.) PHILADELPHIA Cream Cheese, cubed

1 can (14.75 oz.) cream-style corn

2 cups chicken broth

¾ cup milk

2 cups shredded leftover cooked turkey

▶ make it!

1. **COOK** onions and half of the peppers in butter in large saucepan on medium heat until tender, stirring frequently. Reduce heat to low.

2. **ADD** cream cheese; cook until melted, stirring constantly. Add corn, broth, milk and turkey; mix well.

3. **COOK** until soup is heated through, stirring occasionally. Serve topped with remaining peppers.

SPECIAL EXTRA:
For more robust flavor, roast and peel the red bell peppers before chopping; add to the soup along with the turkey. Or, use drained, jarred roasted red peppers instead.

MAKE AHEAD:
Prepare soup as directed; cool. Cover and store in refrigerator up to 48 hours. Reheat before serving.

clam chowder

PREP: 15 min. | TOTAL: 40 min. | MAKES: 5 servings, 1 cup each.

▶ what you need!

1 small onion, chopped

1 stalk celery, chopped

2 slices OSCAR MAYER Bacon, chopped

1 lb. potatoes, peeled, cut into ¼-inch cubes (about 2 cups)

1½ cups water

1 cup milk

4 oz. (½ of 8-oz. pkg.) PHILADELPHIA Cream Cheese, cubed

1 can (6¼ oz.) minced clams, undrained

▶ make it!

1. **COOK** and stir onions, celery and bacon in medium saucepan on medium heat 5 min. or until vegetables are crisp-tender.

2. **ADD** potatoes and water; bring to boil. Cook 15 min. or until potatoes are tender.

3. **MICROWAVE** milk and cream cheese in small microwaveable bowl on HIGH 1½ min. or until milk is heated through. Stir with wire whisk until cream cheese is completely melted. Add to potato mixture; stir until well blended. Stir in the clams with their liquid. Cook 2 min. or until heated through, stirring frequently. (Do not boil.)

cheesy shrimp bisque

PREP: 10 min. | TOTAL: 30 min. | MAKES: 5 servings, 1 cup each.

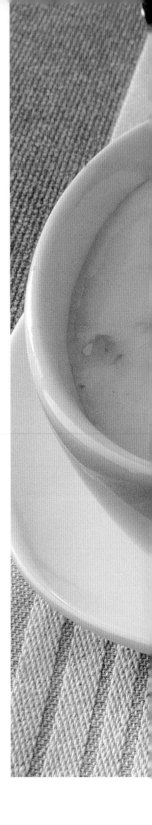

▶ what you need!

½ cup sliced celery

1 Tbsp. butter or margarine

1 pkg. (8 oz.) PHILADELPHIA Cream Cheese, cubed

1 cup milk

½ lb. (8 oz.) VELVEETA Pasteurized Prepared Cheese Product, cut up

1 pkg. (6 oz.) frozen cooked tiny shrimp, thawed, drained

⅓ cup dry white wine

¼ tsp. dill weed

▶ make it!

1. **COOK** and stir celery in butter in 2-qt. saucepan on medium heat until tender. Reduce heat to low.

2. **STIR** in cream cheese and milk; cook until cream cheese is completely melted, stirring occasionally.

3. **ADD** VELVEETA, shrimp and wine; cook until VELVEETA is completely melted and mixture is heated through, stirring occasionally. Sprinkle with dill weed.

HEALTHY LIVING:
Save 80 calories and 11 grams fat per serving by preparing with PHILADELPHIA Neufchâtel Cheese and VELVEETA Made With 2% Milk Reduced Fat Pasteurized Prepared Cheese Product.

VARIATION:
Omit wine. Increase milk to 1⅓ cups.

USE YOUR MICROWAVE:
Decrease milk to ½ cup and wine to ¼ cup. Place celery and butter in 2-qt. microwaveable bowl. Microwave on HIGH 1 to 2 min. or until celery is crisp-tender. Add milk; microwave 3 min., stirring after 2 min. Stir in cream cheese; microwave 4 to 6 min. or until cream cheese is melted, stirring every 2 min. Stir in VELVEETA, shrimp and wine; microwave 2 to 3 min. or until heated through. Sprinkle with dill weed.

creamy zucchini
& spinach rigatoni

PREP. 20 min. | TOTAL. 45 min. | MAKES: 6 servings, 1¼ cups each.

▶ what you need!

8 oz. (½ of 16-oz. pkg.) rigatoni pasta, uncooked

1 tsp. oil

1 zucchini, sliced

½ lb. sliced fresh mushrooms

2 cloves garlic, minced

1 Tbsp. flour

¼ tsp. each dried basil leaves, oregano leaves and crushed red pepper

1 cup fat-free reduced-sodium chicken broth

4 oz. (½ of 8-oz. pkg.) PHILADELPHIA Neufchâtel Cheese, cubed

1 pkg. (6 oz.) baby spinach leaves

¼ cup KRAFT Grated Parmesan Cheese

1½ cups KRAFT Shredded Mozzarella Cheese with a Touch of PHILADELPHIA, divided

▶ make it!

1. **HEAT** oven to 375°F.

2. **COOK** pasta in large saucepan as directed on pkg., omitting salt.

3. **MEANWHILE,** heat oil in large skillet on medium heat. Add zucchini, mushrooms and garlic; cook and stir 3 to 4 min. or until zucchini is crisp-tender. Add flour and seasonings; cook and stir 1 min. Stir in broth; cook and stir 2 to 3 min. or until thickened. Add Neufchâtel; cook and stir 2 to 3 min. or until melted.

4. **DRAIN** pasta; return to pan. Add zucchini mixture, spinach, Parmesan and ½ cup mozzarella; mix lightly. Spoon into 2-qt. casserole sprayed with cooking spray; top with remaining mozzarella.

5. **BAKE** 10 min. or until mozzarella is melted.

SERVING SUGGESTION
Serve with fresh fruit and a side salad to round out the meal.

PREPARING PERFECT PASTA:
Follow the pkg. directions to ensure that enough water is used for cooking the pasta. Add the pasta to the boiling water and cook until al dente (tender but still a little firm to the bite), stirring frequently. To prevent pasta from sticking, add it slowly to plenty of boiling water and stir frequently while cooking. Adding oil to the cooking water is not recommended because some sauces may not cling to pasta coated with oil.

Classic Cheesecakes, Cakes, and Pies

No-fail family favorites

OREO fruit "tart"

PREP: 15 min. | TOTAL: 15 min. | MAKES: 8 servings.

▶ what you need!

- 1 pkg. (8 oz.) PHILADELPHIA Cream Cheese, softened
- ¼ cup sugar
- 2 cups thawed COOL WHIP Whipped Topping
- 1 OREO Pie Crust (6 oz.)
- 2 cups assorted fresh fruit pieces (sliced strawberries, raspberries, blueberries and sliced bananas)
- 4 OREO Cookies, finely chopped
- 2 Tbsp. apricot preserves, melted

▶ make it!

1. **BEAT** cream cheese and sugar in medium bowl with electric mixer on medium speed 1 min. or until well blended. Gently stir in whipped topping.

2. **SPREAD** into pie crust. Top with fruit and chopped cookies; brush fruit with preserves.

3. **REFRIGERATE** until ready to serve. Store leftover tart in refrigerator.

HEALTHY LIVING:
To make a reduced-fat version of this tasty dessert, and save 30 calories per serving too, prepare as directed using PHILADELPHIA Neufchâtel Cheese, COOL WHIP LITE Whipped Topping and OREO Reduced Fat Cookies.

spicy pumpkin cake with chocolate chunks

PREP: 20 min. | TOTAL: 1 hour 30 min. | MAKES: 16 servings, 1 slice each.

▶ what you need!

1 pkg. (2-layer size) spice cake mix

1 pkg. (8 oz.) PHILADELPHIA Cream Cheese, softened, divided

1 cup canned pumpkin

1 tsp. ground cinnamon

½ tsp. ground ginger

6 squares BAKER'S Semi-Sweet Chocolate, coarsely chopped

½ cup thawed COOL WHIP Whipped Topping

2 Tbsp. sugar

▶ make it!

1. **HEAT** oven to 350°F. Prepare cake mix as directed on pkg., reducing water to ½ cup and increasing oil to ½ cup. Add half of the cream cheese, the pumpkin, cinnamon and ginger. Beat on medium speed until well blended. Stir in chopped chocolate. Pour into greased 12-cup fluted tube pan or 10-inch tube pan.

2. **BAKE** 40 to 45 min. or until toothpick inserted in center comes out clean. Cool 10 min. Remove from pan; cool completely on wire rack.

3. **MIX** remaining cream cheese, whipped topping and sugar until well blended. Spread on top of cooled cake. Cut into 16 slices to serve.

SIZE-WISE:
Sweets can be part of a balanced diet, but remember to keep tabs on portions.

SUBSTITUTE:
Substitute yellow cake mix for the spice mix for a less spicy version.

blossoming berry cheesecake

PREP: 25 min. | TOTAL: 5 hours 20 min | MAKES: 16 servings

▶ what you need!

1 cup HONEY MAID Graham Cracker Crumbs

3 Tbsp. sugar

3 Tbsp. butter or margarine, melted

2 eggs, separated

2 pkg. (8 oz. each) PHILADELPHIA Cream Cheese, softened

½ cup sugar

1 tsp. grated lemon peel (optional)

1 Tbsp. lemon juice (optional)

1½ tsp. vanilla, divided

1 cup BREAKSTONE'S or KNUDSEN Sour Cream

2 Tbsp. sugar

1 cup sliced strawberries

½ cup fresh raspberries

▶ make it!

1. **HEAT** oven to 325°F if using a silver 9-inch springform pan (or to 300°F if using a dark nonstick 9-inch springform pan). Mix graham crumbs, 3 Tbsp. sugar and butter; press firmly onto bottom of pan. Bake 10 min.; set aside.

2. **BEAT** egg whites in small bowl with electric mixer on high speed until stiff peaks form; set aside. Beat cream cheese, ½ cup sugar, lemon peel and juice, if desired, and ½ tsp. of the vanilla in large bowl with electric mixer on medium speed until well blended. Add egg yolks, 1 at a time, mixing on low speed after each addition just until blended. Gently stir in egg whites; pour over crust.

3. **BAKE** 45 min. or until center is almost set. Mix sour cream, 2 Tbsp. sugar and remaining 1 tsp. vanilla. Carefully spread over cheesecake. Bake an additional 10 min. Run small knife or metal spatula around rim of pan to loosen cake; cool before removing rim of pan. Refrigerate 4 hours or overnight. Top with strawberries and raspberries just before serving. Store leftover cheesecake in refrigerator.

PARK AVENUE CHEESECAKE:
Omit graham cracker crumbs. Increase sugar for the crust to ⅓ cup and butter to ½ cup. To prepare the crust, beat the ½ cup softened butter or margarine and ⅓ cup sugar with electric mixer on medium speed until light and fluffy. Blend in ¼ tsp. vanilla. Add 1 cup flour; mix well. Reserve ½ cup of the dough; spread remaining dough onto bottom of 9-inch springform pan. Spread reserved ½ cup dough 1¼ inches up side of pan. Bake at 325°F for 10 min.; cool. Prepare cheesecake filling as directed; pour into crust. Bake as directed.

lemon tropical pound cake

PREP: 20 min. | TOTAL: 1 hour 50 min. | MAKES: 12 servings.

▶ what you need!

1 pkg. (8 oz.) PHILADELPHIA Cream Cheese, softened

½ cup butter or margarine, softened

1½ cups granulated sugar

4 eggs

2 cups flour

1½ tsp. CALUMET Baking Powder

1 pkg. (4-serving size) JELL-O Lemon Flavor Gelatin

1½ cups chopped dried fruit (mango, papaya and pineapple), divided

1 cup PLANTERS Chopped Pecans, divided

1 cup powdered sugar

2 Tbsp. lemon juice

▶ make it!

1. **HEAT** oven to 350°F. Beat cream cheese, butter and granulated sugar in large bowl with electric mixer on medium speed until well blended. Add eggs, 1 at a time, mixing well after each addition. Gradually add flour, baking powder and dry gelatin mix, mixing on low speed until well blended. Stir in 1 cup of the dried fruit and ½ cup of the pecans. Pour into greased parchment paper-lined 9-inch square baking pan.

2. **BAKE** 1 hour or until toothpick inserted in center comes out clean and cake is golden brown. Cool 5 min. Invert cake onto wire rack; remove pan. Cool completely.

3. **MIX** powdered sugar and lemon juice; spread over top and sides of cake. Top cake with remaining ½ cup dried fruit and ½ cup pecans.

SIZE-WISE:
You'll know it's a special occasion when you enjoy a serving of this cake!

SUBSTITUTE:
You can substitute a slightly larger size pan for the one called for in the recipe. Try using a 12-cup fluted or 10-inch tube pan, or a 9- or 10-inch round cake pan at least 2 inches deep. Do not use a smaller pan or the batter may run over the top of the pan during baking. Remember that a different pan size affects the baking time (a larger pan may shorten baking times), so check for doneness earlier than the recipe specifies.

mom's easy cake

PREP: 15 min. | TOTAL: 1 hour 45 min. | MAKES: 16 servings.

▶ what you need!

CAKE

  2 squares BAKER'S GERMAN'S Sweet Chocolate

  ½ cup butter or margarine

  1 tsp. vanilla

  1 cup flour

  1 cup granulated sugar

  1 tsp. cream of tartar

  ½ tsp. baking soda

  ½ tsp. salt

  ½ cup milk

  2 eggs

  ½ cup BREAKSTONE'S or KNUDSEN Sour Cream

FROSTING

  4 oz. (½ of 8-oz. pkg.) PHILADELPHIA Cream Cheese, softened

  2 Tbsp. butter or margarine, softened

  ½ tsp. vanilla

  2 cups powdered sugar

  ½ cup BAKER'S ANGEL FLAKE Coconut

  1 square BAKER'S GERMAN'S Sweet Chocolate

  ¼ cup PLANTERS Sliced Almonds

▶ make it!

1. **HEAT** oven to 350°F. Place chocolate squares and butter in top of double boiler or in bowl over a pot of simmering water; heat until chocolate is completely melted. Stir in vanilla. Remove from heat. Mix flour, granulated sugar, cream of tartar, baking soda and salt in large bowl. Add chocolate mixture, milk, eggs and sour cream; mix well. Pour into greased 9-inch square baking pan.

2. **BAKE** 30 to 40 min. or until toothpick inserted in center comes out clean. Cool in pan 5 min. Remove cake from pan; cool completely.

3. **BEAT** cream cheese, butter and vanilla in large bowl with electric mixer on medium speed until well blended. Add powdered sugar gradually, beating until well blended after each addition.

4. **CUT** cake horizontally in half. Spread bottom layer with half of the frosting. Cover with top of cake; spread with remaining frosting. Sprinkle with coconut. Melt chocolate square in microwave as directed on pkg. Sprinkle top of cake with almonds. Drizzle with chocolate. Refrigerate at least 1 hour before serving. Store leftover cake in refrigerator.

CHIPS AHOY!
ice cream cheesecake

PREP: 15 min | TOTAL: 4 hours 15 min | MAKES: 16 servings

▶ what you need!

1 pkg. (15.2 oz.) CHIPS AHOY! Cookies, divided

2 Tbsp. butter, melted

2 pkg. (8 oz. each) PHILADELPHIA Cream Cheese, softened

½ cup sugar

2 tsp. vanilla

1½ qt. (6 cups) vanilla ice cream, slightly softened

▶ make it!

1. **CRUSH** 20 cookies to form fine crumbs; mix with butter until well blended. Press onto bottom of 9-inch springform pan. Chop 16 of the remaining cookies.

2. **BEAT** cream cheese, sugar and vanilla in large bowl with mixer until well blended. Add ice cream; mix well. Stir in chopped cookies; pour over crust.

3. **FREEZE** 4 hours or until firm. Remove from freezer 10 min. before serving; let stand at room temperature to soften slightly. Top with remaining cookies.

SIZE-WISE:
Enjoy your favorite foods on occasion, but keep portion size in mind!

SPECIAL EXTRA:
Drizzle chilled cheesecake with chocolate or caramel sauce, then top each serving with a dollop of thawed COOL WHIP Whipped Topping.

VARIATION:
Prepare in a 13×9-inch pan instead of the springform pan.

NILLA praline cheesecake

PREP: 20 min. | TOTAL: 6 hours 5 min. | MAKES: 16 servings.

▶ what you need!

66 NILLA Wafers, divided

1¼ cups sugar, divided

¼ cup margarine or butter, melted

3 pkg. (8 oz. each) PHILADELPHIA Cream Cheese, softened

½ cup BREAKSTONE'S or KNUDSEN Sour Cream

1 tsp. vanilla

3 eggs

25 KRAFT Caramels

3 Tbsp. milk

½ cup PLANTERS Pecan Pieces, toasted

▶ make it!

1. **HEAT** oven to 325°F. Finely crush 50 wafers; mix with ¼ cup sugar and margarine. Press onto bottom of 9-inch springform pan. Stand remaining wafers around edge, pressing gently into crust to secure.

2. **BEAT** cream cheese and remaining sugar in large bowl with mixer until well blended. Add sour cream and vanilla; mix well. Add eggs, 1 at a time, beating on low speed after each just until blended. Pour over crust.

3. **BAKE** 45 to 50 min. or until center is almost set. Run small knife around rim of pan to loosen cake; cool before removing rim. Refrigerate 4 hours. Microwave caramels and milk on HIGH 1 min. or until caramels are completely melted, stirring every 30 sec. Cool slightly. Pour over cheesecake; top with nuts.

SUBSTITUTE:
Line 13×9-inch pan with foil, with ends of foil extending over sides. Grease foil. Prepare recipe as directed, increasing whole NILLA Wafers around the side from 16 to 22. Bake 40 to 45 min. or until center is almost set. Use foil handles to lift dessert from pan before cutting into squares to serve.

NOTE:
If using a dark nonstick 9-inch springform pan, reduce oven temperature to 300°F.

HOW TO TOAST NUTS:
Toasting nuts adds crunch and intensifies their flavor. To toast nuts in the oven, spread nuts in single layer in shallow baking pan. Bake at 350°F for 10 to 15 min. or until golden brown, stirring occasionally.

PHILADELPHIA blintz cake

PREP: 15 min. | TOTAL: 1 hour | MAKES: 12 servings.

▶ what you need!

3 eggs, divided

1 pkg. (8 oz.) PHILADELPHIA Cream Cheese, softened

1 cup BREAKSTONE'S or KNUDSEN Cottage Cheese

¾ cup sugar, divided

½ cup butter, softened

¾ cup milk

1 tsp. vanilla

1¼ cups flour

1 tsp. CALUMET Baking Powder

1 cup blueberry pie filling

▶ make it!

1. **HEAT** oven to 350°F.

2. **BEAT** 1 egg, cream cheese, cottage cheese and ¼ cup sugar with whisk until well blended; set aside.

3. **ADD** butter and remaining sugar to large bowl; beat with mixer until light and fluffy. Beat in remaining eggs, milk and vanilla. Add combined flour and baking powder; beat until well blended. Pour half the batter into greased shallow 2-qt. baking dish. Carefully spread cream cheese mixture over batter in dish; top with layers of pie filling and remaining batter.

4. **BAKE** 45 min. or until puffed and lightly browned.

SIZE-WISE:
You'll know it's a special occasion when you get to enjoy a serving of this delicious cake!

SUBSTITUTE:
Prepare using apple pie filling.

german chocolate cheesecake

PREP: 30 min. | TOTAL: 5 hours 30 min. | MAKES: 14 servings.

▶ what you need!

1 cup finely crushed FAMOUS Chocolate Wafers

1 cup sugar, divided

3 Tbsp. butter or margarine, melted

3 pkg. (8 oz. each) PHILADELPHIA Cream Cheese, softened

¼ cup flour

1 pkg. (4 oz.) BAKER'S GERMAN'S Sweet Chocolate, melted

2½ tsp. vanilla, divided

4 eggs, divided

⅓ cup canned evaporated milk

¼ cup butter or margarine

½ cup BAKER'S ANGEL FLAKE Coconut

½ cup PLANTERS Chopped Pecans

▶ make it!

1. **HEAT** oven to 350°F if using a silver 9-inch springform pan (or to 325°F if using a dark nonstick 9-inch springform pan). Mix chocolate wafer crumbs, 2 Tbsp. of the sugar and 3 Tbsp. butter; press firmly onto bottom of pan. Bake 10 min.

2. **BEAT** cream cheese, ½ cup of the sugar and the flour in large bowl with electric mixer on medium speed until well blended. Add chocolate and 2 tsp. of the vanilla; mix well. Add 3 of the eggs, 1 at a time, mixing on low speed after each addition just until blended. Pour over crust.

3. **BAKE** 45 to 50 min. or until center is almost set. Run knife or metal spatula around rim of pan to loosen cake; cool before removing rim of pan. Refrigerate 4 hours or overnight.

4. **PLACE** evaporated milk, remaining sugar, the ¼ cup butter, remaining egg and remaining ½ tsp. vanilla in small saucepan; cook on medium-low heat until thickened, stirring constantly. Stir in coconut and pecans. Cool. Spread over cheesecake just before serving. Store leftover cheesecake in refrigerator.

SIZE-WISE:
Since this indulgent special-occasion dessert makes 14 servings, it is a perfect dessert to serve at your next party.

PHILADELPHIA vanilla mousse cheesecake

PREP: 30 min. | TOTAL: 6 hours 15 min. | MAKES: 16 servings.

▶ what you need!

40 NILLA Wafers, crushed (about 1½ cups)

3 Tbsp. butter or margarine, melted

4 pkg. (8 oz. each) PHILADELPHIA Cream Cheese, softened, divided

1 cup sugar, divided

1 Tbsp. plus 1 tsp. vanilla, divided

3 eggs

1 tub (8 oz.) COOL WHIP Whipped Topping, thawed

▶ make it!

1. **HEAT** oven to 325°F.

2. **MIX** wafer crumbs and butter; press onto bottom of 9-inch springform pan.

3. **BEAT** 3 pkg. cream cheese, ¾ cup sugar and 1 Tbsp. vanilla with mixer until well blended. Add eggs, 1 at a time, mixing on low speed after each just until blended. Pour over crust.

4. **BAKE** 50 to 55 min. or until center is almost set. Run knife around rim of pan to loosen cake; cool completely in pan.

5. **BEAT** remaining cream cheese, sugar and vanilla with mixer in large bowl until well blended. Whisk in COOL WHIP; spread over cheesecake. Refrigerate 4 hours. Remove rim of pan before serving cheesecake.

SIZE-WISE:
Need a sweet treat to serve a crowd? Try this rich, creamy dessert! Since it serves 16 people, it easily fits the bill.

VANILLA BEAN MOUSSE CHEESECAKE:
Prepare recipe as directed, using a vanilla bean and reducing vanilla extract to 2 tsp. Use sharp knife to gently split 1 vanilla bean pod lengthwise in half, then scrape seeds into cheesecake batter. Add 1 tsp. vanilla extract to the batter and use remaining extract to flavor cheesecake topping as directed.

SPECIAL EXTRA:
Garnish with fresh berries just before serving.

PHILADELPHIA blueberry crown cheesecake

PREP: 15 min. | TOTAL: 5 hours 15 min. | MAKES: 16 servings.

▶ what you need!

30 NILLA Wafers, crushed (about 1 cup)

1 cup plus 3 Tbsp. sugar, divided

3 Tbsp. butter or margarine, melted

5 pkg. (8 oz. each) PHILADELPHIA Cream Cheese, softened

3 Tbsp. flour

1 Tbsp. vanilla

   Grated peel from 1 medium lemon

1 cup BREAKSTONE'S or KNUDSEN Sour Cream

4 eggs

2 cups fresh blueberries

▶ make it!

1. **HEAT** oven to 325°F if using a silver 9-inch springform pan (or to 300°F if using a dark nonstick 9-inch springform pan). Mix wafer crumbs, 3 Tbsp. of the sugar and butter until well blended. Press firmly onto bottom of pan.

2. **BEAT** cream cheese, remaining 1 cup sugar, flour, vanilla and lemon peel with electric mixer on medium speed until well blended. Add sour cream; mix well. Add eggs, 1 at a time, beating on low speed after each addition just until blended. Pour over crust; top with blueberries.

3. **BAKE** 1 hour 10 min. to 1 hour 15 min. or until center is almost set. Run small knife or spatula around rim of pan to loosen cake; cool before removing rim of pan. Refrigerate at least 4 hours before serving. Store leftover cheesecake in refrigerator.

SIZE IT UP:
Savor a serving of this crowd-pleasing dessert on special occasions.

SPECIAL EXTRA:
Garnish with additional blueberries and fresh mint sprigs just before serving.

GREAT SUBSTITUTE:
Substitute 1 bag (16 oz.) thawed frozen blueberries or 1 can (15 oz.) blueberries, well drained, for the 2 cups fresh blueberries.

PHILADELPHIA
classic cheesecake

PREP: 20 min | TOTAL: 5 hours 45 min | MAKES: 16 servings

▶ what you need!

1½ cups HONEY MAID Graham Cracker Crumbs

3 Tbsp. sugar

⅓ cup butter or margarine, melted

4 pkg. (8 oz. each) PHILADELPHIA Cream Cheese, softened

1 cup sugar

1 tsp. vanilla

4 eggs

▶ make it!

1. **HEAT** oven to 325°F.

2. **MIX** graham crumbs, 3 Tbsp. sugar and butter; press onto bottom of 9-inch springform pan.

3. **BEAT** cream cheese, 1 cup sugar and vanilla with mixer until well blended. Add eggs, 1 at a time, mixing on low speed after each just until blended. Pour over crust.

4. **BAKE** 55 min. or until center is almost set. Loosen cake from rim of pan; cool before removing rim. Refrigerate 4 hours.

SIZE-WISE:
Sweets can add enjoyment to a balanced diet, but remember to keep tabs on portions.

SPECIAL EXTRA:
Top with fresh fruit just before serving.

ribbon bar cheesecake

PREP: 15 min. | TOTAL: 5 hours 15 min. | MAKES: 16 servings, 1 square each.

▶ what you need!

30 OREO Chocolate Sandwich Cookies, crushed

½ cup butter, melted

¼ cup PLANTERS Chopped Pecans

¼ cup BAKER'S ANGEL FLAKE Coconut

4 pkg. (8 oz. each) PHILADELPHIA Cream Cheese, softened

1 cup sugar

4 eggs

½ cup whipping cream

6 squares BAKER'S Semi-Sweet Chocolate

▶ make it!

1. **HEAT** oven to 350°F. Mix cookie crumbs, butter, pecans and coconut; press firmly onto bottom of 13×9-inch baking pan. Refrigerate while preparing filling.

2. **BEAT** cream cheese and sugar in large bowl with electric mixer on medium speed until well blended. Add eggs, 1 at a time, mixing on low speed after each addition just until blended. Pour over crust.

3. **BAKE** 40 min. or until center is almost set. Cool. Refrigerate 3 hours or overnight. Place whipping cream and chocolate in saucepan. Cook on low heat until chocolate is completely melted and mixture is well blended, stirring occasionally. Pour over cheesecake. Refrigerate 15 min. or until chocolate is firm. Store leftover cheesecake in refrigerator.

chocolate silk pie with marshmallow meringue

PREP: 15 min. | TOTAL: 2 hours 15 min. | MAKES: 10 servings.

▶ what you need!

5 squares BAKER'S Bittersweet Chocolate, divided

4 oz. (½ of 8-oz. pkg.) PHILADELPHIA Cream Cheese, softened

1 jar (7 oz.) JET-PUFFED Marshmallow Creme, divided

1 pkg. (3.9 oz.) JELL-O Chocolate Instant Pudding

1 cup milk

1 OREO Pie Crust (6 oz.)

1 cup thawed COOL WHIP Whipped Topping

▶ make it!

1. **MICROWAVE** 4 chocolate squares in medium microwaveable bowl on HIGH 1 to 1½ min. or until melted, stirring after 1 min. Add cream cheese, ½ of marshmallow creme, dry pudding mix and milk; beat with mixer until well blended. Spoon into crust.

2. **BEAT** remaining marshmallow creme and COOL WHIP in separate bowl until well blended. Spread over chocolate layer in crust.

3. **REFRIGERATE** 2 hours or until firm. Use remaining chocolate square to make chocolate curls; arrange on pie.

SIZE-WISE:
Since this special-occasion dessert makes enough to feed a crowd, it makes a great dessert to serve at your next party or family gathering.

HOW TO MAKE CHOCOLATE CURLS:
Microwave chocolate square on HIGH a few sec. or just until you can smudge chocolate with your thumb. Pull a vegetable peeler slowly along bottom of square to make curl. Repeat to make additional curls.

frozen coconut pie

PREP: 15 min. | TOTAL: 4 hours 15 min. | MAKES: 8 servings.

▶ what you need!

4 oz. (½ of 8-oz. pkg.) PHILADELPHIA Cream Cheese, softened

1 Tbsp. sugar

½ cup milk

1 cup BAKER'S ANGEL FLAKE Coconut

1 tub (8 oz.) COOL WHIP or COOL WHIP Extra Creamy Whipped Topping, thawed

½ tsp. almond or vanilla extract

1 HONEY MAID Graham Pie Crust (6 oz.)

▶ make it!

1. **BEAT** cream cheese and sugar in large bowl with electric mixer on medium speed until well blended. Gradually add milk, beating until well blended after each addition.

2. **STIR** in coconut, COOL WHIP and extract. Spoon into crust.

3. **FREEZE** 4 hours or until firm. Remove pie from freezer about 15 min. before serving. Let stand at room temperature until pie can be cut easily. Store leftover pie in freezer.

SIZE-WISE:
Enjoy a serving of this rich-and-indulgent treat on special occasions.

USE YOUR BLENDER:
Place cream cheese, sugar and milk in blender container; cover. Blend on low speed 30 sec.; spoon into medium bowl. Gently stir in coconut, whipped topping and extract. Spoon into crust and continue as directed.

HOW TO SOFTEN CREAM CHEESE:
Place completely unwrapped pkg. of cream cheese in microwaveable bowl. Microwave on HIGH 15 to 20 sec. or just until softened. Add 15 sec. for each additional pkg. of cream cheese.

PHILADELPHIA blueberry no-bake cheesecake

PREP: 15 min. | TOTAL: 4 hours 15 min. | MAKES: 16 servings

▶ what you need!

2 cups HONEY MAID Graham Cracker Crumbs

6 Tbsp. margarine, melted

1 cup sugar, divided

4 pkg. (8 oz. each) PHILADELPHIA Neufchâtel Cheese, softened

½ cup blueberry preserves

Grated peel from 1 lemon

1 pkg. (16 oz.) frozen blueberries, thawed, drained

1 tub (8 oz.) COOL WHIP LITE Whipped Topping, thawed

▶ make it!

1. **MIX** graham crumbs, margarine and ¼ cup of the sugar; press firmly onto bottom of 13×9-inch pan. Refrigerate while preparing filling.

2. **BEAT** Neufchâtel cheese and remaining ¾ cup sugar in large bowl with electric mixer on medium speed until well blended. Add preserves and lemon peel, mix until blended. Stir in blueberries. Gently stir in COOL WHIP. Spoon over crust; cover.

3. **REFRIGERATE** 4 hours or until firm. Garnish as desired. Store leftovers in refrigerator.

HOW TO MAKE IT WITH FRESH BLUEBERRIES:
Place 2 cups blueberries in small bowl with 2 Tbsp. sugar; mash with fork. Add to Neufchâtel cheese mixture; continue as directed.

layered pineapple-lemon cheesecake pie

PREP: 15 min. | TOTAL: 3 hours 15 min. | MAKES: 10 servings.

▶ what you need!

1 pkg. (8 oz.) PHILADELPHIA Cream Cheese, softened

¼ cup sugar

2 cups thawed COOL WHIP Whipped Topping

1 can (8 oz.) crushed pineapple, drained, divided

1 HONEY MAID Graham Pie Crust (6 oz.)

1 pkg. (3.4 oz.) JELL-O Lemon Flavor Instant Pudding

1⅓ cups cold milk

▶ make it!

1. **BEAT** cream cheese and sugar in large bowl with whisk until well blended. Stir in COOL WHIP and half the pineapple.

2. **SPREAD** into crust.

3. **BEAT** pudding mix and milk in medium bowl with whisk 2 min. (Mixture will be thick.) Stir in remaining pineapple. Spoon over pie. Refrigerate 3 hours or until chilled.

HEALTHY LIVING:
Save 90 calories and 8 grams of fat per serving by preparing with PHILADELPHIA Neufchâtel Cheese, COOL WHIP LITE Whipped Topping, a ready-to-use reduced-fat graham cracker crumb crust, fat-free milk and JELL-O Vanilla Flavor Fat Free Sugar Free Instant Pudding.

SUBSTITUTE:
Prepare using a NILLA Pie Crust.

chocolate PHILADELPHIA tunnel cake

PREP. 10 min. | TOTAL. 55 min. | MAKES. 10 servings.

▶ what you need!

2 pkg. (8 oz. each) PHILADELPHIA Cream Cheese, softened

¼ cup granulated sugar

1 egg

2 tsp. vanilla, divided

1 pkg. (2-layer size) chocolate cake mix

1 cup powdered sugar

2 oz. (¼ of 8-oz. pkg.) PHILADELPHIA Cream Cheese, softened

2 Tbsp. milk

▶ make it!

1. **HEAT** oven to 350°F. Grease and flour 12-cup fluted tube pan or 10-inch tube pan. Beat 2 pkg. cream cheese, the granulated sugar, egg and 1 tsp. of the vanilla in medium bowl with electric mixer on medium speed until well blended; set aside.

2. **PREPARE** cake batter as directed on pkg.; pour half of the batter into prepared pan. Spoon cream cheese mixture in ring around center of cake batter; cover with remaining cake batter.

3. **BAKE** 45 min. or until toothpick inserted near center comes out clean. Cool in pan on wire rack 30 min. Loosen cake from side of pan; invert onto serving platter. Cool completely.

4. **BEAT** remaining 1 tsp. vanilla, the powdered sugar, 2 oz. cream cheese and the milk with wire whisk until well blended. Drizzle over cake. Let stand until set.

SIZE-WISE:
Savor a serving of this indulgent special-occasion dessert. And since it serves 16 people, it makes a great dessert to serve at your next party!

VARIATION:
To make cupcakes instead, line 24 medium muffin cups with paper liners. Prepare cake batter and cream cheese mixture as directed. Spoon ¼ cup of the batter into each cup; top with 1 Tbsp. of the cream cheese mixture and an additional ¼ cup cake batter. Bake 20 to 22 min. or until wooden toothpick inserted in centers comes out clean. Cool 10 min. Remove from pans. Makes 24 servings, 1 cupcake each.

Chocolate Delights

Recipes featuring everyone's favorite flavor

chocolate-caramel creme pie

PREP: 30 min. | **TOTAL: 3 hours 30 min.** | **MAKES: 8 servings.**

▶ what you need!

18 OREO Cookies, finely crushed (about 1½ cups)

3 Tbsp. butter, melted

4 oz. (½ of 8-oz. pkg.) PHILADELPHIA Cream Cheese, softened

2 Tbsp. caramel ice cream topping

1 cup thawed COOL WHIP Whipped Topping

1 pkg. (3.9 oz.) JELL-O Chocolate Instant Pudding

1½ cups cold milk

▶ make it!

1. **COMBINE** cookie crumbs and butter; press onto bottom and up side of 9-inch pie plate sprayed with cooking spray. Refrigerate until ready to use.

2. **MIX** cream cheese and caramel topping in medium bowl until well blended. Gently stir in COOL WHIP; spread onto bottom of crust.

3. **BEAT** pudding mix and milk with whisk 2 min.; pour over cream cheese layer. Refrigerate 3 hours.

SIZE-WISE:
Enjoy a serving of this rich-and-indulgent treat on special occasions.

warm & gooey peanut butter-chocolate cake

PREP: 15 min. | TOTAL: 45 min. | MAKES: 16 servings

▶ what you need!

1 pkg. (2-layer size) chocolate cake mix

½ cup butter, melted

4 eggs, divided

1 pkg. (8 oz.) PHILADELPHIA Cream Cheese, softened

½ cup creamy peanut butter

2 cups powdered sugar

▶ make it!

1. **HEAT** oven to 350°F.

2. **BEAT** cake mix, butter and 2 eggs with mixer on low speed 30 sec., stopping frequently to scrape beater and side of bowl. Beat on medium speed 2 min. Spread onto bottom of 13×9-inch pan sprayed with cooking spray.

3. **BEAT** remaining ingredients until well blended; pour over batter in pan.

4. **BAKE** 30 min. or until edges are firm. Cool slightly.

SIZE-WISE:
Since this indulgent cake makes 16 servings, it is the perfect dessert to serve at your next party!

KEEPING IT SAFE:
Refrigerate any leftovers.

SUBSTITUTE:
Swap in your favorite flavor of cake mix to change up the flavor.

chocolate-banana heaven cake

PREP: 20 min. | TOTAL: 55 min. | MAKES: 16 servings.

▶ what you need!

1 pkg. (2-layer size) chocolate cake mix (not pudding in the mix variety)

½ cup cocoa powder

1 cup prepared MAXWELL HOUSE Instant Coffee, cooled

4 medium ripe bananas, mashed

3 eggs

⅓ cup water

1 tsp. MAXWELL HOUSE Instant Coffee

2 Tbsp. milk, warmed

1 pkg. (8 oz.) PHILADELPHIA Cream Cheese, softened

3 squares BAKER'S Semi-Sweet Chocolate, melted

2 cups powdered sugar

½ cup PLANTERS Chopped Pecans

▶ make it!

1. **HEAT** oven to 350°F. Grease and flour 2 (9-inch) round cake pans. Cover bottoms of pans with waxed paper; set aside.

2. **COMBINE** cake mix and cocoa powder in large bowl. Add the prepared coffee, bananas, eggs and water; beat with electric mixer on low speed 30 sec., stopping frequently to scrape bottom and side of bowl. Beat on medium speed 2 min.; pour evenly into prepared pans.

3. **BAKE** 30 to 35 min. or until toothpick inserted in centers comes out clean. Cool 10 min.; remove from pans to wire racks. Immediately remove waxed paper. Cool cake layers completely.

4. **DISSOLVE** 1 tsp. instant coffee in the warm milk. Beat cream cheese with electric mixer on medium speed until creamy. Add milk mixture; beat 2 min. Blend in melted chocolate. Add powdered sugar; beat until light and fluffy. Use to fill and frost cooled cake layers. Immediately press pecans into frosting on side of cake. Garnish with chocolate curls, if desired.

SIZE-WISE:
Enjoy a serving of this indulgent treat on special occasions.

VARIATION:
Prepare as directed, substituting muffin pans for the round cake pans. Spoon batter evenly into 24 paper-lined medium muffin cups, filling each cup two-thirds full. Bake at 350°F for 25 to 30 min. or until wooden toothpick inserted in centers comes out clean. Cool completely on wire racks before spreading with frosting. Makes 2 doz. or 24 servings, 1 cupcake each.

HOW TO MAKE CHOCOLATE CURLS:
Melt 2 squares BAKER'S Semi-Sweet or White Chocolate as directed on pkg. Spread into very thin layer on baking sheet. Refrigerate 10 min. or until chocolate is firm, but still pliable. To make curls, push a metal spatula firmly onto bottom of baking sheet, under the chocolate, so the chocolate curls as it is pushed. (If chocolate is too firm, let stand a few min. at room temperature; refrigerate again if it becomes too soft.)

choco-cherry bars

PREP: 30 min. | TOTAL: 1 hour | MAKES: 36 servings.

▶ what you need!

4 squares BAKER'S Unsweetened Chocolate, divided

1 pkg. (8 oz.) PHILADELPHIA Cream Cheese, softened

¾ cup butter or margarine, softened

1 cup granulated sugar

2 eggs

1½ tsp. vanilla, divided

1¼ cups flour

½ tsp. baking soda

½ tsp. salt

1 cup chopped maraschino cherries, well drained

½ cup chopped PLANTERS Walnuts

1 cup powdered sugar

2 to 3 Tbsp. milk, divided

▶ make it!

1. **HEAT** oven to 350°F. Melt 2 chocolate squares; set aside. Beat cream cheese, butter and granulated sugar in large bowl with mixer until blended. Add eggs and 1 tsp. vanilla; mix well. Mix flour, baking soda and salt. Add to cream cheese mixture; mix well. Blend in melted chocolate. Stir in cherries and nuts.

2. **SPREAD** into greased and floured 15×10×1-inch pan.

3. **BAKE** 25 to 30 min. or until toothpick inserted in center comes out clean. Melt remaining chocolate squares in medium microwaveable bowl. Stir in powdered sugar, 2 Tbsp. milk and remaining vanilla. Add remaining 1 Tbsp. milk, if necessary, for desired glaze consistency. Drizzle over dessert. Cool completely.

chocolate cake roll

PREP: 20 min. | TOTAL: 2 hours 5 min. | MAKES: 10 servings.

▶ what you need!

6 squares BAKER'S Semi-Sweet Chocolate, divided

6 Tbsp. butter

1 cup granulated sugar

4 eggs

1 cup flour, divided

½ tsp. baking soda

⅔ cup water

¾ cup powdered sugar, divided

4 oz. (½ of 8-oz. pkg.) PHILADELPHIA Cream Cheese, softened

3 cups thawed COOL WHIP Whipped Topping, divided

▶ make it!

1. **HEAT** oven to 350°F.

2. **SPRAY** 15×10×1-inch pan with cooking spray. Line with waxed paper; spray with additional cooking spray.

3. **MICROWAVE** 3 chocolate squares and butter in medium microwaveable bowl on HIGH 1½ to 2 min. or until butter is melted. Stir until chocolate is completely melted. Add granulated sugar; mix well. Beat eggs in large bowl with mixer on high speed 3 min. or until thickened. Blend in chocolate mixture. Add ¼ cup flour and baking soda; beat just until blended. Add remaining flour alternately with water, beating well after each addition. Spread evenly into prepared pan.

4. **BAKE** 15 min. or until top of cake springs back when touched; sprinkle with ¼ cup powdered sugar. Immediately invert cake onto clean towel; remove pan. Carefully peel off paper. Starting at 1 short side, roll up cake and towel together; cool completely on wire rack.

5. **BEAT** cream cheese and remaining powdered sugar in medium bowl with mixer until well blended. Gently stir in 1½ cups COOL WHIP.

6. **UNROLL** cake carefully; remove towel. Spread cream cheese mixture onto cake, completely covering top of cake. Roll up cake; place, seam-side down, on platter.

7. **MICROWAVE** remaining chocolate and remaining COOL WHIP in microwaveable bowl on HIGH 1 to 1½ min. or until chocolate is completely melted and mixture is well blended, stirring after 1 min. Cool 2 min.; spread onto cake. Refrigerate 1 hour.

SIZE-WISE:
Enjoy a serving of this crowd-pleasing dessert on special occasions.

NOTE:
Don't worry if the cake cracks when it is unrolled. The creamy frosting will cover the cracks beautifully.

SPECIAL EXTRA:
Sprinkle frosted cake with additional 1 Tbsp. sifted powdered sugar just before serving.

chocolate-orange layer cake

PREP: 20 min. | TOTAL: 20 min. | MAKES: 16 servings.

▶ what you need!

1½ pkg. (8 oz. each) PHILADELPHIA Cream Cheese, softened

6 Tbsp. butter, softened

6 cups powdered sugar

1 Tbsp. orange peel

12 drops orange food coloring

2 baked chocolate cake layers (8 inch), cooled

3 squares BAKER'S Semi-Sweet Chocolate

½ cup (½ of 8-oz. tub) COOL WHIP Whipped Topping (Do not thaw.)

▶ make it!

1. **BEAT** first 5 ingredients with mixer until well blended.

2. **CUT** each cake horizontally into 2 layers. Stack on plate, spreading ¾ cup frosting between each layer. Frost top and side with remaining frosting.

3. **MICROWAVE** chocolate and COOL WHIP in microwaveable bowl on HIGH 2 min. or until chocolate is completely melted and mixture is well blended, stirring after each minute. Cool 15 min.; spread over top of cake, allowing excess to drizzle down side. Keep refrigerated.

SIZE-WISE:
The orange flavor is a perfect complement to the chocolate in this special-occasion cake.

SUBSTITUTE:
Substitute 8 drops yellow and 4 drops red food coloring for the orange food coloring.

chocolate-raspberry mousse

PREP: 25 min. | TOTAL: 2 hours 25 min. | MAKES: 16 servings.

▶ what you need!

15 OREO Cookies, finely crushed (about 1½ cups)

2 Tbsp. butter, melted

2 cups fresh raspberries

1 pkg. (8 squares) BAKER'S Semi-Sweet Chocolate, divided

2 pkg. (8 oz. each) PHILADELPHIA Cream Cheese, softened

1 can (14 oz.) sweetened condensed milk

2 cups thawed COOL WHIP Whipped Topping, divided

▶ make it!

1. **MIX** cookie crumbs and butter; press onto bottom of 9-inch springform pan. Reserve 12 raspberries; spread remaining raspberries over crust.

2. **MELT** 7 chocolate squares as directed on pkg.; set aside. Beat cream cheese in large bowl with mixer until creamy. Add condensed milk; mix well. Add melted chocolate; beat until well blended. Whisk in 1 cup COOL WHIP; spoon over raspberry layer in pan. Freeze 2 hours.

3. **RUN** knife around rim of pan to loosen dessert; remove rim. Cut 8 of the reserved raspberries in half. Garnish dessert with remaining COOL WHIP, halved berries and remaining whole berries. Melt remaining chocolate square; drizzle over dessert. Let stand until firm.

VARIATION:
Prepare as directed using 1 pkg. (6 squares) BAKER'S White Chocolate, using all 6 of the chocolate squares in the mousse filling and omitting the chocolate drizzle garnish.

SIZE-WISE:
You'll know it's a special occasion when you get to enjoy a serving of this delicious mousse!

VARIATION:
To serve as a chilled dessert, refrigerate dessert 4 hours or until firm instead of freezing it. For a make-ahead dessert, refrigerate dessert up to 24 hours before serving.

strawberry truffle brownies

PREP: 20 min. | TOTAL: 1 hour 55 min. | MAKES: 20 servings, 1 brownie each.

▶ what you need!

1½ pkg. (12 squares) BAKER'S Semi-Sweet Chocolate, divided

½ cup butter

1 tsp. MAXWELL HOUSE Instant Coffee

¾ cup firmly packed light brown sugar

2 eggs

¾ cup flour

½ tsp. CALUMET Baking Powder

1 pkg. (8 oz.) PHILADELPHIA Cream Cheese, softened

½ cup strawberry jam

¼ cup powdered sugar

▶ make it!

1. **HEAT** oven to 350°F. Line 9-inch square baking pan with foil, with ends of foil extending over sides of pan; grease foil. Place 10 of the chocolate squares, the butter and instant coffee in large microwaveable bowl. Microwave on HIGH 2 min. or until butter is melted. Stir until chocolate is completely melted. Add brown sugar and eggs; mix well. Stir in flour and baking powder. Spread into prepared pan.

2. **BAKE** 30 to 35 min. or until toothpick inserted in center comes out with fudgy crumbs. Cool in pan on wire rack.

3. **PLACE** remaining 2 chocolate squares in large microwaveable bowl. Microwave on HIGH 1 min.; stir until completely melted. Add cream cheese; beat with electric mixer on medium speed until well blended. Add jam and powdered sugar; beat on low speed until well blended. Spread over cooled brownie. Refrigerate at least 1 hour or until topping is set. Cut into 20 bars. Store leftover brownies in tightly covered container in refrigerator.

SIZE-WISE:
This interesting twist on a traditional brownie recipe makes a special treat. One batch makes enough to serve 20!

SUBSTITUTE:
Prepare as directed, using 1½ cups BAKER'S Semi-Sweet Chocolate Chunks.

PHILADELPHIA triple-chocolate cheesecake

PREP: 20 min. | TOTAL: 5 hours 45 min. | MAKES: 16 servings.

▶ what you need!

24 OREO Cookies, crushed (about 2 cups)

2 Tbsp. butter or margarine, melted

1 pkg. (6 squares) BAKER'S White Chocolate, divided

4 pkg. (8 oz. each) PHILADELPHIA Cream Cheese, softened, divided

1 cup sugar, divided

½ tsp. vanilla

3 eggs

3 squares BAKER'S Semi-Sweet Chocolate, divided

1 tub (8 oz.) COOL WHIP Whipped Topping, thawed

▶ make it!

1. **HEAT** oven to 325°F.

2. **MIX** cookie crumbs and butter; press onto bottom of 9-inch springform pan. Melt 5 white chocolate squares as directed on pkg.; cool slightly.

3. **BEAT** 3 pkg. cream cheese, ¾ cup sugar and vanilla with mixer until well blended. Add melted white chocolate; mix well. Add eggs, 1 at a time, mixing on low speed after each just until blended. Pour over crust.

4. **BAKE** 50 to 55 min. or until center is almost set. Run knife around rim of pan to loosen cake; cool completely. Meanwhile, melt 2 semi-sweet chocolate squares; cool.

5. **BEAT** remaining cream cheese and sugar in large bowl until well blended. Add melted semi-sweet chocolate; mix well. Whisk in COOL WHIP; spread over cheesecake. Refrigerate 4 hours. Garnish with chocolate curls from remaining white and semi-sweet chocolates.

SIZE-WISE:
Need a sweet treat to serve a crowd? Try this chocolatey dessert! Since it serves 16 people, it easily fits the bill.

VARIATION:
Substitute foil-lined 13×9-inch pan for the springform pan. Mix crust ingredients as directed. Press onto bottom of prepared pan; cover with prepared filling. Bake 45 min. or until center is almost set. Cool

completely in pan. Spread with COOL WHIP mixture. Refrigerate 4 hours. Use ends of foil to remove cheesecake from pan before cutting to serve.

HOW TO SHAVE CHOCOLATE:
Warm 1 chocolate square by microwaving it on HIGH for a few sec. or just until you can smudge the chocolate with your thumb. Hold square steadily, then draw a vegetable peeler slowly over the chocolate to form shavings. Repeat with remaining chocolate square.

white chocolate cheesecake

PREP: 30 min. | TOTAL: 6 hours 30 min. | MAKES: 16 servings.

▶ what you need!

¾ cup sugar, divided

½ cup butter, softened

1½ tsp. vanilla, divided

1 cup flour

4 pkg. (8 oz. each) PHILADELPHIA Cream Cheese, softened

2 pkg. (6 squares each) BAKER'S White Chocolate, melted, slightly cooled

4 eggs

1 pt. (2 cups) raspberries and chopped fresh mint (optional)

▶ make it!

1. **HEAT** oven to 325°F if using a silver 9-inch springform pan (or to 300°F if using a dark nonstick 9-inch springform pan). Beat ¼ cup of the sugar, the butter and ½ tsp. of the vanilla in small bowl with electric mixer on medium speed until light and fluffy. Gradually add flour, mixing on low speed until well blended after each addition. Press firmly onto bottom of pan; prick with fork. Bake 25 min. or until edge is lightly browned.

2. **BEAT** cream cheese, remaining ½ cup sugar and remaining 1 tsp. vanilla in large bowl with electric mixer on medium speed until well blended. Add melted chocolate; mix well. Add eggs, 1 at a time, beating on low speed after each addition just until blended. Pour over crust.

3. **BAKE** 1 hour or until center is almost set. Run knife or metal spatula around rim of pan to loosen cake; cool before removing rim of pan. Refrigerate 4 hours or overnight. Top with the raspberries and mint, if desired, just before serving. Store leftover cheesecake in refrigerator.

silky chocolate cheesecake

PREP: 15 min. | TOTAL: 5 hours 10 min. | MAKES: 12 servings.

▶ what you need!

1¾ cups OREO Chocolate Cookie Crumbs

2 Tbsp. sugar

⅓ cup butter or margarine, melted

2 pkg. (4 oz. each) BAKER'S GERMAN'S Sweet Chocolate, divided

2 eggs

⅔ cup corn syrup

⅓ cup whipping cream

1½ tsp. vanilla

2 pkg. (8 oz. each) PHILADELPHIA Cream Cheese, cubed, softened

▶ make it!

1. **HEAT** oven to 325°F if using a silver 9-inch springform pan (or to 300°F if using a dark nonstick 9-inch springform pan). Mix cookie crumbs, sugar and butter until well blended. Press firmly onto bottom and 1½ inches up side of pan. Microwave 1½ pkg. (6 squares) of the chocolate in microwaveable bowl on HIGH 2 min., stirring after 1 min. Stir until chocolate is completely melted.

2. **PLACE** eggs, corn syrup, whipping cream and vanilla in blender container; cover. Blend until smooth. With blender running, gradually add cream cheese through small opening at top of blender, blending until smooth. Add melted chocolate; cover. Blend well. Pour into crust.

3. **BAKE** 50 to 55 min. or until center is almost set. Run knife or metal spatula around rim of pan to loosen cake; cool before removing from pan. Refrigerate 4 hours or overnight.

4. **MELT** remaining 2 squares of chocolate as directed on pkg. Drizzle over cheesecake just before serving. Store leftover cheesecake in refrigerator.

creamy chocolate bars

PREP: 20 min. | TOTAL: 4 hours 20 min. | MAKES: 18 servings, 1 bar each.

▶ what you need!

30 squares HONEY MAID Chocolate Grahams, divided

2 pkg. (8 oz. each) PHILADELPHIA Cream Cheese, softened

3 cups milk

3 pkg. (4-serving size each) JELL-O Chocolate Instant Pudding

1 tub (8 oz.) COOL WHIP Whipped Topping, thawed

▶ make it!

1. **ARRANGE** 15 grahams on bottom of 13×9-inch pan, cutting to fit if necessary.

2. **BEAT** cream cheese in bowl with mixer until smooth. Gradually beat in 1 cup milk until blended. Add remaining milk and dry pudding mixes; beat on low speed for 2 min. Gently stir in COOL WHIP.

3. **SPREAD** half the pudding mixture in prepared pan. Top with remaining grahams and pudding mixture. Refrigerate for at least 4 hours or overnight.

4. **CUT** into 18 bars.

SIZE-WISE:
An occasional dessert can be a part of a balanced diet, but remember to keep tabs on portions.

SPECIAL EXTRA:
Garnish with fresh raspberries.

so-easy german chocolate cake

PREP: 10 min. | TOTAL: 40 min. | MAKES: 16 servings.

▶ what you need!

1 pkg. (19.5 oz.) brownie mix

¼ cup butter, cut up

4 oz. (½ of 8-oz. pkg.) PHILADELPHIA Cream Cheese, cubed

½ cup firmly packed brown sugar

1 cup BAKER'S ANGEL FLAKE Coconut

1 cup PLANTERS Pecan Pieces

▶ make it!

1. **HEAT** oven to 350°F. Prepare brownie mix as directed on pkg. for cake-like brownies. Pour batter into greased 13×9-inch baking pan.

2. **PLACE** butter and cream cheese in small saucepan; cook on medium heat until cream cheese is completely melted and mixture is well blended, stirring frequently. Stir in sugar. Add coconut and pecans; mix well. (Mixture will be thick.) Drop spoonfuls of the cream cheese mixture over brownie batter in pan.

3. **BAKE** 30 min. or until toothpick inserted in center comes out clean. Cool 1 hour. Store leftover cake in the refrigerator.

EASY CLEANUP:
Make cleanup easier by lining baking pan with foil before using. To easily remove the baked cake from pan, extend foil beyond sides of pan. Then use the foil as handles to remove the cake from the pan.

SIZE-WISE:
A serving of this special-occasion dessert goes a long way on flavor.

our best chocolate cheesecake

PREP: 30 min. | TOTAL: 5 hours 35 min. | MAKES: 16 servings.

▶ what you need!

18 OREO Cookies, crushed (about 1½ cups)

2 Tbsp. butter or margarine, melted

3 pkg. (8 oz. each) PHILADELPHIA Cream Cheese, softened

1 cup sugar

1 tsp. vanilla

1 pkg. (8 squares) BAKER'S Semi-Sweet Chocolate, melted, slightly cooled

3 eggs

1 cup thawed COOL WHIP Whipped Topping

1½ cups assorted seasonal fruit, such as chopped strawberries and sliced kiwi

▶ make it!

1. **HEAT** oven to 325°F if using a silver 9-inch springform pan (or to 300°F if using a dark nonstick 9-inch springform pan). Mix crushed cookies and butter; press firmly onto bottom of pan. Bake 10 min.

2. **BEAT** cream cheese, sugar and vanilla with electric mixer on medium speed until well blended. Add chocolate; mix well. Add eggs, 1 at a time, mixing on low speed after each addition just until blended. Pour over crust.

3. **BAKE** 45 to 55 min. or until center is almost set. Run knife or metal spatula around rim of pan to loosen cake; cool before removing rim of pan. Refrigerate 4 hours or overnight. Top with COOL WHIP and fruit.

HOW TO:
This recipe can also be made in a greased, foil-lined 13×9-inch baking pan. Reduce the baking time by 5 to 10 min.

SIZE-WISE:
Looking for a special treat? One serving of this cheesecake is full of chocolatey flavor.

kansas city mud pie

PREP: 1 hour | TOTAL: 4 hours | MAKES: 16 servings, 1 slice each.

▶ what you need!

1¼ cups finely chopped PLANTERS Pecans

¾ cup flour

¼ cup butter or margarine, melted

2 pkg. (8 oz. each) PHILADELPHIA Cream Cheese, softened

1½ cups powdered sugar

1 tub (8 oz.) COOL WHIP Whipped Topping, thawed, divided

2⅔ cups cold milk

2 pkg. (4-serving size each) JELL-O Chocolate Flavor Instant Pudding & Pie Filling

▶ make it!

1. **HEAT** oven to 375°F. Mix pecans, flour and butter; press onto bottom of 9-inch springform pan. Bake 20 min. Cool.

2. **BEAT** cream cheese and sugar with electric mixer until well blended. Gently stir in 1½ cups COOL WHIP; spread over crust. Beat milk and dry pudding mixes with wire whisk 2 min. or until well blended. Spoon over cream cheese layer.

3. **REFRIGERATE** 3 hours or until set. Run knife or metal spatula around rim of pan to loosen dessert; remove rim. Top pie with remaining COOL WHIP just before serving. Store leftovers in refrigerator.

   JAZZ IT UP:
   Drizzle each serving plate with 1 Tbsp. raspberry sauce before topping with pie slice.

chocolate bliss cheesecake

PREP: 20 min. | TOTAL: 6 hours | MAKES: 12 servings.

▶ what you need!

18 OREO Cookies, crushed (about 1½ cups)

2 Tbsp. butter or margarine, melted

3 pkg. (8 oz. each) PHILADELPHIA Cream Cheese, softened

¾ cup sugar

1 tsp. vanilla

1 pkg. (8 squares) BAKER'S Semi-Sweet Chocolate, melted, cooled slightly

3 eggs

▶ make it!

1. **HEAT** oven to 325°F.

2. **MIX** cookie crumbs and butter; press onto bottom of 9-inch springform pan.

3. **BEAT** cream cheese, sugar and vanilla with mixer until well blended. Add chocolate; mix well.

4. **ADD** eggs, 1 at a time, mixing on low speed after each just until blended. Pour over crust.

5. **BAKE** 55 min. to 1 hour or until center is almost set. Run knife around rim of pan to loosen cake; cool before removing rim. Refrigerate 4 hours.

SPECIAL EXTRA:
Garnish with powdered sugar and fresh raspberries just before serving.

prize winning chocolate cheesecake

PREP: 20 min. | TOTAL: 1 hour 20 min. | MAKES: 10 servings.

▶ what you need!

¾ cup PLANTERS Sliced Almonds, finely chopped

1½ cups TEDDY GRAHAMS Chocolate Graham Snacks, crushed

¼ cup butter, melted

1 tsp. vanilla, divided

2 pkg. (8 oz. each) PHILADELPHIA Cream Cheese, softened

½ cup sugar

1 jar (13 oz.) chocolate-hazelnut spread

1 tub (8 oz.) COOL WHIP or COOL WHIP Extra Creamy Whipped Topping, thawed

▶ make it!

1. **MIX** nuts, graham crumbs, butter and ½ tsp. vanilla; press onto bottom and up side of 9-inch pie plate. Refrigerate until ready to use.

2. **BEAT** cream cheese and sugar in large bowl with mixer until well blended. Add hazelnut spread and remaining vanilla; mix well. Gently stir in COOL WHIP. Spoon into crust.

3. **REFRIGERATE** 4 hours before serving.

SIZE-WISE:
This sensational cheesecake is full of flavor. And since it makes 10 servings, it can feed a crowd at your next gathering or family party.

HOW TO SOFTEN CREAM CHEESE:
Place completely unwrapped pkg. of cream cheese in microwaveable bowl. Microwave on HIGH 15 to 20 sec. or just until softened. Add 15 sec. for each additional pkg. of cream cheese.

PHILADELPHIA no-bake chocolate cherry cheesecake

PREP: 10 min. | TOTAL: 3 hours 10 min. | MAKES: 10 servings.

▶ what you need!

2 pkg. (8 oz. each) PHILADELPHIA Cream Cheese, softened

1 pkg. (4 oz.) BAKER'S GERMAN'S Sweet Chocolate, melted, cooled

⅓ cup sugar

1 tub (8 oz.) COOL WHIP Whipped Topping, thawed

1 HONEY MAID Graham Pie Crust (6 oz.)

1 can (21 oz.) cherry pie filling

▶ make it!

1. **BEAT** cream cheese, chocolate and sugar in large bowl with electric mixer on medium speed until well blended. Gently stir in COOL WHIP.

2. **SPOON** into crust.

3. **REFRIGERATE** 3 hours or overnight. Top with pie filling just before serving. Store leftover cheesecake in refrigerator.

cookies & cream freeze

PREP: 30 min. | TOTAL: 3 hours 30 min. | MAKES: 12 servings, 1 piece each.

▶ what you need!

- 4 squares BAKER'S Semi-Sweet Chocolate
- 14 OREO Cookies, divided
- 1 pkg. (8 oz.) PHILADELPHIA Cream Cheese, softened
- ¼ cup sugar
- ½ tsp. vanilla
- 1 tub (8 oz.) COOL WHIP Whipped Topping, thawed

▶ make it!

1. **MELT** chocolate as directed on pkg.; set aside until ready to use. Line 8½×4½-inch loaf pan with foil, with ends of foil extending over sides of pan. Arrange 8 of the cookies evenly on bottom of pan. Crumble remaining 6 cookies; set aside.

2. **BEAT** cream cheese, sugar and vanilla in medium bowl with electric mixer until well blended. Stir in COOL WHIP. Remove about 1½ cups of the cream cheese mixture; place in medium bowl. Stir in melted chocolate.

3. **SPREAD** remaining cream cheese mixture over cookies in pan; sprinkle with crumbled cookies. Gently press cookies into cream cheese mixture with back of spoon; top with chocolate mixture. Cover. Freeze 3 hours or until firm. Remove from freezer about 15 min. before serving; invert onto serving plate. Peel off foil; let stand at room temperature to soften slightly before cutting to serve.

SPECIAL EXTRA:
Drizzle serving plates with additional melted BAKER'S Semi-Sweet Chocolate for a spectacular, yet simple, dessert presentation.

SIZE-WISE:
Sweets can be part of a balanced diet, but remember to keep tabs on portions.

CHIPS AHOY!
cheesecake sandwiches

PREP: 10 min. | TOTAL: 3 hours 10 min. | MAKES: 10 servings, 1 sandwich each.

▶ what you need!

4 oz. (½ of 8-oz. pkg.) PHILADELPHIA Cream Cheese, softened

2 Tbsp. sugar

1 cup thawed COOL WHIP Whipped Topping

20 CHIPS AHOY! Real Chocolate Chip Cookies

1 tub (7 oz.) BAKER'S Real Milk Dipping Chocolate, melted

▶ make it!

1. **BEAT** cream cheese and sugar in large bowl with electric mixer on medium speed until well blended. Stir in COOL WHIP.

2. **COVER** bottom (flat) side of each of 10 of the cookies with about 2 Tbsp. of the cream cheese mixture; top each with second cookie, bottom-side down, to form sandwich. Dip half of each sandwich in chocolate; gently shake off excess chocolate. Place in single layer in airtight container.

3. **FREEZE** 3 hours or until firm. Store leftover sandwiches in freezer.

index

D

E

F

METRIC CONVERSION CHART

VOLUME MEASUREMENTS (dry)

1/8 teaspoon = 0.5 mL
1/4 teaspoon = 1 mL
1/2 teaspoon = 2 mL
3/4 teaspoon = 4 mL
1 teaspoon = 5 mL
1 tablespoon = 15 mL
2 tablespoons = 30 mL
1/4 cup = 60 mL
1/3 cup = 75 mL
1/2 cup = 125 mL
2/3 cup = 150 mL
3/4 cup = 175 mL
1 cup = 250 mL
2 cups = 1 pint = 500 mL
3 cups = 750 mL
4 cups = 1 quart = 1 L

VOLUME MEASUREMENTS (fluid)

1 fluid ounce (2 tablespoons) = 30 mL
4 fluid ounces (1/2 cup) = 125 mL
8 fluid ounces (1 cup) = 250 mL
12 fluid ounces (1 1/2 cups) = 375 mL
16 fluid ounces (2 cups) = 500 mL

WEIGHTS (mass)

1/2 ounce = 15 g
1 ounce = 30 g
3 ounces = 90 g
4 ounces = 120 g
8 ounces = 225 g
10 ounces = 285 g
12 ounces = 360 g
16 ounces = 1 pound = 450 g

DIMENSIONS

1/16 inch = 2 mm
1/8 inch = 3 mm
1/4 inch = 6 mm
1/2 inch = 1.5 cm
3/4 inch = 2 cm
1 inch = 2.5 cm

OVEN TEMPERATURES

250°F = 120°C
275°F = 140°C
300°F = 150°C
325°F = 160°C
350°F = 180°C
375°F = 190°C
400°F = 200°C
425°F = 220°C
450°F = 230°C

BAKING PAN SIZES

Utensil	Size in Inches/Quarts	Metric Volume	Size in Centimeters
Baking or Cake Pan (square or rectangular)	8×8×2	2 L	20×20×5
	9×9×2	2.5 L	23×23×5
	12×8×2	3 L	30×20×5
	13×9×2	3.5 L	33×23×5
Loaf Pan	8×4×3	1.5 L	20×10×7
	9×5×3	2 L	23×13×7
Round Layer Cake Pan	8×1½	1.2 L	20×4
	9×1½	1.5 L	23×4
Pie Plate	8×1¼	750 mL	20×3
	9×1¼	1 L	23×3
Baking Dish or Casserole	1 quart	1 L	—
	1½ quarts	1.5 L	—
	2 quarts	2 L	—